19
43
97
75
103
105
109

By Diane Wakoski

The Motorcycle Betrayal Poems
The Magellanic Clouds
Inside the Blood Factory
The George Washington Poems
Discrepancies and Apparitions
Coins and Coffins

THE MOTORCYCLE BETRAYAL POEMS

DIANE WAKOSKI

SIMON AND SCHUSTER · NEW YORK

Second printing
SBN 671-21011-4
Library of Congress Catalog Card Number: 74–156164
Designed by Eve Metz
Manufactured in the United States of America by
· American Book–Stratford Press, New York

Permission to reprint the following poems that have previously appeared in the publications listed below is gratefully acknowledged: "I Have Had to Learn to Live With My Face," copyright © 1970, and "The Lament of the Lady Bank Dick," copyright © 1969 by Diane Wakoski, first published in **Caterpillar** (the latter title also published by Sans Souci Press); "Love Letter Postmarked Van Beethoven," copyright © 1969, and "Film: Called 5 Blind Men," copyright © 1970 by Diane Wakoski, first published in **Sumac**; "Bloodroot," copyright © 1969 by Diane Wakoski, first published in **Grain**; "My Hell's Angel," copyright © 1969, and "Indian Giver," copyright © 1969 by Diane Wakoski, first published in **Noose**; "Thanking My Mother for Piano Lessons," copyright © 1969 by Diane Wakoski, first published by Perishable Press; "Anticipation of Sharks," copyright © 1971 by Diane Wakoski, first published in **Armadillo**; "The Moon Has a Complicated Geography," copyright © 1969 by Diane Wakoski, first published in **The Moon Has a Complicated Geography**, by Odda Tala Press; "I Lay Next to You All Night, Trying Awake to Understand the Watering Place of the Moon," copyright © 1969, and "Sunflowers in My Wrist," copyright © 1969 by Diane Wakoski, first published in **Stony Brook Journal**; "No More Soft Talk," copyright © 1969 by Diane Wakoski, first published in **New American Review**; "Five Love Poems," copyright © 1969 by Diane Wakoski, first published in **Kayak**; "The Ten-Dollar Cab Ride," copyright © 1970 by Diane Wakoski, first published in **Lillibulero**; "With Words," copyright © 1968 by Diane Wakoski, first published in **Works** (also included in **The Moon Has a Complicated Geography**, published by Odda Tala Press, copyright © 1969); "Black Leather Because Bumblebees Look Like It," copyright © 1962 by Diane Wakoski, first published in **Four Young Lady Poets** by Totem-Corinth; "To Celebrate My Body," copyright © 1968 by Diane Wakoski, first published in **The Young American Poets** by Follett Publishing Co.; "Caves," copyright © 1970 by Diane Wakoski, first published in **Concerning Poetry**.
   The quotations on pages 75–79 come from poems in the anthology **Five Blind Men**.

This book is dedicated to all those men
who betrayed me at one time or another,
in hopes they will fall off their motorcycles
and break their necks.

CONTENTS

THE MOTORCYCLE BETRAYAL POEMS

I HAVE HAD TO LEARN TO LIVE WITH MY FACE

You see me alone tonight.
My face has betrayed me again,
    the garage mechanic who promises to fix my car
    and never does.

My face
that my friends tell me is so full of character;
my face
I have hated for so many years;
my face
I have made an angry contract to live with
though no one could love it;
my face that I wish you would bruise and batter
and destroy, napalm it, throw acid in it,
so that I might have another
or be rid of it at last.

I drag peacock feathers behind me
to erase the trail of the moon. Those tears
I shed for myself,
sometimes in anger.
There is no pretense in my life. The man who lives with me
must see something beautiful,

like a dark snake coming out of my mouth,
or love the tapestry of my actions, my life/ this body, this
face, they have nothing to offer
but angry insistence, their presence.
I hate them,
want my life to be more.
Hate their shadow on even my words.

11

I sell my soul for good plumbing
and hot water,
                I tell everyone;
and my face is soft,
opal,
a feathering of snow
against the
            cold black leather coat
which is night.
                You,
                night,
                my face against the chilly
                expanse
                of your back.
Learning to live with what you're born with
is the process,
the involvement,
the making of a life.
And I have not learned happily
to live with my face,
that Diane which always looks better on film
than in life.
I sternly accept this plain face,
and hate every moment of that sternness.

I want to laugh at this ridiculous face
        of lemon rinds
        and vinegar cruets
        of unpaved roads
        and dusty file cabinets
        of the loneliness of Wall Street at night
        and the desert of school on a holiday
but I would have to laugh alone in a cold room
Prefer the anger
that at least for a moment gives me a proud profile.

Always, I've envied
        the rich
            the beautiful
            the talented
                the go-getters
                of the world. I've watched
myself
remain
alone
isolated
a fish that swam through the net
because I was too small
        but remained alone
        in deep water because the others were caught
        taken away
It is so painful for me to think now,
to talk about this; I want to go to sleep and never wake up.
The only warmth I ever feel is wool covers on a bed.
But self-pity could trail us all, drag us around on the bottom of
shoes like squashed snails so that
we might never fight/ and it is anger I want now, fury,
to direct at my face and its author,
to tell it how much I hate what it's done to me,
to contemptuously, sternly, brutally even, make it live with itself,
look at itself every day,
and remind itself
that reality is
learning to live with what you're born with,
noble to have been anything but defeated,
that pride and anger and silence will hold us above beauty,
though we bend down often with so much anguish for
a little beauty,
a word, like the blue night,
        the night of rings covering the floor and glinting
        into the fire, the water, the wet earth, the age of songs,

guitars, angry busloads of etched tile faces, old gnarled
tree trunks, anything with the beauty of wood, teak, lemon,
cherry
I lost my children because I had no money, no husband,
I lost my husband because I was not beautiful,
I lost everything a woman needs, wants,
almost
before I became a woman,
my face shimmering and flat as the moon
with no features.

I look at pictures of myself as a child.
I looked lumpy, unformed, like a piece of dough,
and it has been my task as a human being
to carve out a mind, carve out a face,
carve out a shape with arms & legs, to put a voice inside,
and to make a person from a presence.
And I don't think I'm unique.
I think a thousand of you, at least, can look at those old photos,
reflect on your life
and see your own sculpture at work.

I have made my face as articulate as I can,
and it turns out to be a peculiar face with too much
bone in the bridge of the nose, small eyes, pale lashes,
thin lips, wide cheeks, a rocky chin,
But it's almost beautiful compared to the sodden mass of dough I
started out with.

I wonder how we learn to live
with our faces?
They must hide so much pain,
so many deep trenches of blood,
so much that would terrorize and drive others away, if they
could see it. The struggle to control it

articulates the face.
And what about those people
With elegant noses and rich lips?

What do they spend their lives struggling for?

Am I wrong I constantly ask myself
to value the struggle
more than the results?
Or only to accept a beautiful face
if it has been toiled for?

Tonight I move alone in my face;
want to forgive all the men whom I've loved
who've betrayed me.
After all, the great betrayer is that one I carry around each day,
which I sleep with at night. My own face,
angry building I've fought to restore
imbued with arrogance, pride, anger and scorn.
To love this face
would be to love a desert mountain,
a killer, rocky, water hard to find, no trees anywhere/
perhaps I do not expect anyone
to be strange enough to love it;
but you.

LOVE LETTER POSTMARKED VAN BEETHOVEN

for a man I love
more than I should,
intemperance being something
a poet cannot afford

I am too angry to sleep beside you,
you big loud symphony who fell asleep drunk;
I try to count sheep and instead
find myself counting the times I would like to shoot you
in the back,
your large body
with its mustaches that substitute for love
and its knowledge of motorcycle mechanics that substitutes
for loving me;
why aren't you interested in
my beautiful little engine?
It needs a tune-up tonight, dirty with the sludge of
anger, resentment,
and the pistons all sticky, the valves
afraid of the lapping you might do,
the way you would clean me out of your life.

I count the times your shoulders writhe
and you topple over
after I've shot you with my Thompson Contender
    (using the .38-caliber barrel
     or else the one they recommend for shooting rattlesnakes).
I shoot you each time in that wide dumb back,
insensitive to me,
glad for the mild recoil of the gun
that relieves a little of my repressed anger
each time I discharge a bullet into you;
one for my father who deserted me and whom you masquerade as,
every night, when you don't come home

or even telephone to give me an idea of when to expect you;
the anguish of expectation in one's life
and the hours when the mind won't work, waiting
for the sound of footsteps on the stairs,
the key turning in the lock;
another bullet for my first lover,
a boy of 18
     (but that was when I was 18 too)
who betrayed me and would not marry me.
You too, betrayer,
you who will not give me your name as even a token of affection;
another bullet,
and of course each time
the heavy sound of your body falling over in heavy shoes
a lumber jacket, and a notebook in which you write down
everything
but reality;
another bullet for those men
who said they loved me
and followed other women into their silky bedrooms
and kissed them behind curtains,
who offered toasts to other women,
making me feel ugly, undesirable;
anger, fury, the desire to cry or to shake you back
to the way you used to love me,
even wanted to,
knowing that I have no recourse,
that if I air my grievances you'll only punish me more
or tell me to leave,
and yet knowing that silent grievances
will erode my brain,
make pieces of my ability to love
fall off,
like fingers from a leprosied hand;
and I shoot another bullet into your back,

trying to get to sleep,
only wanting you to touch me with some gesture of affection;
this bullet for the bad husband who would drink late in bars
and not take me with him,
talking and flirting with other women,
and who would come home, without a friendly word, and sleep
celibate next to my hungry body;
a bullet for the hypocrites;
a bullet for my brother who could not love me without guilt;
a bullet for the man I love who never listens to me;
a bullet for the men who run my country without consulting me;
a bullet for the man who says I am a fool to expect anyone to listen
                                    to me;
a bullet for the man who wrote a love poem to me
and a year later threw it away, saying it was a bad poem;
If I were Beethoven, by now I'd have tried every
dissonant chord;
were I a good marksman, being paid to test this new Thompson
Contender, I'd have several dozen dead rattlers lying
along this path already;
instead, I am ashamed of my anger
at you
whom I love
whom I ask for so much more than you want to give.
A string quartet would be too difficult right now.
Let us have the first movement of the Moonlight Sonata
I will try counting the notes
instead of sheep.

UNEASY RIDER

Falling in love with a mustache
is like saying
you can fall in love with
the way a man polishes his shoes
          which,
          of course,
          is one of the things that turns on
          my tuned-up engine

          those trim buckled boots

          (I feel like an advertisement
          for men's fashions
          when I think of your ankles)

Yeats was hung up with a girl's beautiful face

and I find myself

a bad moralist,

a failing aesthetician,

a sad poet,

wanting to touch your arms and feel the muscles
that make a man's body have so much substance,
that makes a woman
lean and yearn in that direction
that makes her melt/ she is a rainy day
in your presence

the pool of wax under a burning candle
the foam from a waterfall

You are more beautiful than any Harley-Davidson
She is the rain,
waits in it for you,
finds blood spotting her legs
from the long ride.

BLOODROOT

Bloodroot,
white flower in my throat
dripping from its stem
the iodine plasma
of its name,

you are growing under all the trees,
transfusing me this spring.
I am in love with the motorcyclist
but he betrays me
with the moon.

Artificial flowers,
that I imagine,
Black Bloodroot,
ride by
on their motorcycles
betraying me also.
Betraying me
in their leather jackets studded
with iron butterflies,
but I have leaped
on needled feet
out of the ground.
My soft covered white face
whispers and smiles,
reminds me of my life: profuse as the Bloodroot drops
growing at every tree base.
In spite of your winter betrayals,
I hold myself,
tall,
my 2 inches
above ground would fill some poet's eyes. I hold myself better

21

than you could hold me,
Motorcyclist,
black man. Bloodroot
who passes me without any face or hands.
Without any roots.
Without blood
for my new life.

THE DESERT MOTORCYCLIST

Road as wide open
as my shoulders when I am loving
the tides
the dry sand that blows against you like rain—
I am riding away from you:
away from your voice that troubles me,
like a leak in the basement,
away from your timidities
about frogs and salamanders,
away down this desert road,
purple and bloody with dusk.

Pools of the afternoon spray me,
distorting your image.
You caged me in water,
imprisoned me in tide pools/ remembering I am the spiny starfish,
softer inside than evolution should allow.

Now I run away
to my dry desert,
the place where there is enough space
for my imagination
and nothing to drown it.

Desert motorcyclist:
that is me.
And it is always the man,
never the machine
who betrays me.

MY HELL'S ANGEL

This will be a straightforward poem.
This will have no beautiful sidetracking, like flutes on a shell,
to distract you.
This will have no digressions,
>   like wet fern,
>   like kelp dragging your feet down in water
>   like ground glass between your teeth
>   like ornamented crosses and velvet coats
>   like rusty pistols
>   or crusty bread
to disguise my feelings,
to silhouette and forget me.

This will be a poem without imaginary characters
a point in time, an encounter,
a poetic moment,
someone else talking,
without an elegant race horse
to distract you.

I am writing it
because I had an experience that was a poem.
Because I am a romantic
Because my life is unfulfilled and I am looking for
new experiences
Because I open myself up to poetry
Because everyone talks it
when they see how very well
I listen.

This year.
Now.
Summer.

24

Beach. Where I am. A lonely woman
Ripe, exotic, with a grace
few women have.
Infectious smile. Friendly. Open.
Warm if I like you.
Walking on the beach
I have heard poetry. I am expecting to see people.
There are two hours of sunset on the beach
and I go down to walk on it,
to see the tide come up high against the rocks and swirl
like my favorite paintings around
my feet.
I have forgotten all the men I love.
I remember that I am alone
But I have lots of things to do.
And I am wearing my purple bikini
with a crinkly white shirt over it because it is a cool sunset.
Cool sunset
remember that.

I walk down the beach. It is
empty.
I am thinking of the men I love.
I have forgotten the men I love.
They are blond.
They are dark.
They all have mustaches,
ride motorcycles,
mainly exist in my head.

Against the rocks,
in the last strong rays of sunlight
I see a man in levis,
with his shirt off,
a beard, longish hair,

he is relaxed into the rocks,
a part of the beach. Beside him
are motorcycle boots, which he is not wearing.
I like men who ride motorcycles.
I like the way his levis fit.
I am an old Californian.
The beach turns me on.
I decide he is someone I would like to interest.
I walk out into the foam.
I play in the water.
I skirt him. I am a skirt,
but I am wearing a bikini. My legs are tan.
I have long hair. It blows in the sunset, the salty air.
My dark glasses give me the look of an ancient scarab.

He gets up and walks over to where I am playing
into the waves. He is small.
Very muscular. The kind of man I like,
with a straight nose. Scars, many scars on his
shirtless torso. I am already participating in a literary event.
He is a character in my sunset-on-the-beach play. I am curious
what he will say and do. I like him because I have created him
and then by accident found him there.

He asks me if I live here and I say no, I am here for the summer.
I ask him if he lives here and he says no, his bike is broken and
is in San Diego and he is staying here until he can get it fixed.

I know then that he doesn't just wear motorcycle boots.
He rides motorcycles. His arm is tattooed.
It says, "Apache."

He asks me
referring to the two gold loops in my pierced ears,
if I have another earring.

Laughing I say, no, why should I have three earrings.
I like to laugh. It is part of the sunset.
Part of a play. Part of the deepness I feel in my body
about being alive. I can always cry or laugh. I
can reach down and pull out the creased edges of my body this way.
I am in touch with the water. It laps my feet.
Sun glints off my eyeglasses. I am
happy to be alive. Happy to encounter life.

He asks me if I will give him one of my earrings.
What would I do with only one, I ask him, laughing again,
happy that there are people like me who ask for what they want
and really expect the world to give it to them.
He doesn't even answer such a silly question. Obviously
whatever I do with only one earring is my business, not his.
It is gold. It shines in my ear.
It reminds me of the man who pierced my ears.
It reminds me of my pierced heart, of a car called Pierce Arrow,
it reminds me that the sun is glinting off my smile,
that the small waves are around my feet and I'm talking to a man
with one hole in one ear, wearing levis, who rides a broken Harley,
on a beach at sunset in California
and that there is nothing in my life
but the sun glinting off my earring and that the earring
could be given away and nothing would change.
An ex-
change.
No change.
So I take the earring from my left ear, and I laugh
and I hand it to him.

He puts it in his ear.

Now I tell him I am a poet.
And he tells me about his life.

27

It is a life of challenge. He wants to challenge every man
to fight him. He wants to prove his body against every man.

He rides with the Angels he tells me,
and he tells me of fishing,
of hunting with only a knife,
of riding,
of the pleasure of being a longshoreman when he has to work,
of moving his body in the cold,
of comparing what he can do with men much taller and bigger
                              than he,
he tells me of loading tuna on the icy boats, of only wearing his
T-shirt, he tells me of sleeping on the beach at night, of the
challenge of riding his bike in winter on the sleety streets, of
the wind of Chicago. His eye
has a scar in it. He fights men who offer to buy him a beer
and make fun of his beard. He is blond,
he wants to fight the world off,
I do not want to fight the world off, but I love
this stranger, with my gold earring glinting in his ear
wanting to fight off the world,
to prove he is half Apache,
born on the reservation in Arizona,
riding with a gang of men who talk poetry.

Where are my roots, I ask myself,
scarcely getting a word into this monologue,
the man who talks like an angel,
rides with the angels,
and whom I will see this once on a sunset beach in California.
I look at the cliffs over the beach.
We talk about building houses.
He knows how to fight,
and to construct buildings.

The ice plant is dry, barely holds in the eroding cliffs.
California will fall into the ocean soon.
He won't be sleeping on a cliff or under it when California does this.

He likes the Black Panther, he tells me.
I laugh.
Ask him which ones.
He does not understand me.
We talk about the elegance of big cats.
This one is special he says. He would like to own one.
My only monologue is delivered then
on the beach
in the sunset,
the tide getting higher,
one ear empty of its gold, my hands
moving like a cat pawing at my long hair
which moves in the salty beach air.

Why do you want to own the panther, I say.
Aren't you contradicting everything you've told me about being
wild and loving things for their wildness, wanting everything
to be free, wanting to fight for everything, to prove who is
freest, who in control?
Why must you own it?
Why must anyone own something to love it?
Why can't you let it come and go?
I am so afraid of owning things and tell him

but he knows
because I've given him my gold earring
and someone who cared about his possessions
would not give such a thing casually away.

I gave it because I knew that it was part of the encounter,
the exchange,
that everything we have is that way.

The tide got so high, he had to pick up his jacket, his wrist watch
and run. He was waiting to meet his girl friend. We ran
to where we might find his girl friend. She came, I walked away.
It was nice talking to you, I said,
laughing,
walking away, exhilarated,
knowing there are people whose will to survive
gives them muscles far beyond their size.
I will always remember
his muscles,
his Apache tattoo,
his words about the joy of fighting and winning,
the sadness of his broken bike,
his candor in immediately asking for what he wanted,
the sun on the beach,
my hair blowing,
the sun on my face,
the tide around my ankles,
the sun on his straight nose,
the eroding cliffs,
his anger at people who wouldn't fight, who had no pride,
the sun glinting on my gold earrings,
the sun on the gold hair on my arm,
the sun glinting off the waves,
the sun which he'd wake up to in the morning, on the beach,
the sun he put in my heart
because he was so alive
and he shared some of it
with me.

THANKING MY MOTHER FOR PIANO LESSONS

The relief of putting your fingers on the keyboard,
as if you were walking on the beach
and found a diamond
as big as a shoe;

as if
you had just built a wooden table
and the smell of sawdust was in the air,
your hands dry and woody;

as if
you had eluded
the man in the dark hat who had been following you
all week;

the relief
of putting your fingers on the keyboard,
playing the chords of
Beethoven,
Bach,
Chopin
  in an afternoon when I had no one to talk to,
  when the magazine advertisement forms of soft sweaters
  and clean shining Republican middle-class hair
  walked into carpeted houses
  and left me alone
  with bare floors and a few books

I want to thank my mother
for working every day
in a drab office
in garages and water companies
cutting the cream out of her coffee at 40

to lose weight, her heavy body
writing its delicate bookkeeper's ledgers
alone, with no man to look at her face,
her body, her prematurely white hair
in love
       I want to thank
my mother for working and always paying for
my piano lessons
before she paid the Bank of America loan
or bought the groceries
or had our old rattling Ford repaired.

I was a quiet child,
afraid of walking into a store alone,
afraid of the water,
the sun,
the dirty weeds in back yards,
afraid of my mother's bad breath,
and afraid of my father's occasional visits home,
knowing he would leave again;
afraid of not having any money,
afraid of my clumsy body,
that I knew
        no one would ever love

But I played my way
on the old upright piano
obtained for $10,
played my way through fear,
through ugliness,
through growing up in a world of dime-store purchases,
and a desire to love
a loveless world.

I played my way through an ugly face
and lonely afternoons, days, evenings, nights,
mornings even, empty
as a rusty coffee can,
played my way through the rustles of spring
and wanted everything around me to shimmer like the narrow tide
on a flat beach at sunset in Southern California,
I played my way through
an empty father's hat in my mother's closet
and a bed she slept on only one side of,
never wrinkling an inch of
the other side,
waiting,
waiting,

I played my way through honors in school,
the only place I could
talk
 the classroom,
 or at my piano lessons, Mrs. Hillhouse's canary always
 singing the most for my talents,
 as if I had thrown some part of my body away upon entering
 her house
 and was now searching every ivory case
 of the keyboard, slipping my fingers over black
 ridges and around smooth rocks,
 wondering where I had lost my bloody organs,
 or my mouth which sometimes opened
 like a California poppy, wide and with contrasts
 beautiful in sweeping fields,
 entirely closed morning and night,

I played my way from age to age,
but they all seemed ageless
or perhaps always

old and lonely,
wanting only one thing, surrounded by the dusty bitter-smelling
leaves of orange trees,
wanting only to be touched by a man who loved me,
who would be there every night
to put his large strong hand over my shoulder,
whose hips I would wake up against in the morning,
whose mustaches might brush a face asleep,
dreaming of pianos that made the sound of Mozart
and Schubert without demanding
that life suck everything
out of you each day,
without demanding the emptiness
of a timid little life.

I want to thank my mother
for letting me wake her up sometimes at 6 in the morning
when I practiced my lessons
and for making sure I had a piano
to lay my school books down on, every afternoon.
I haven't touched the piano in 10 years,
perhaps in fear that what little love I've been able to
pick, like lint, out of the corners of pockets,
will get lost,
slide away,
into the terribly empty cavern of me
if I ever open it all the way up again.
Love is a man
with a mustache
gently holding me every night,
always being there when I need to touch him;
he could not know the painfully loud
music from the past that
his loving stops from pounding, banging,
battering through my brain,

which does its best to destroy the precarious gray matter when I
am alone;
he does not hear Mrs. Hillhouse's canary singing for me,
liking the sound of my lesson this week,
telling me,
confirming what my teacher says,
that I have a gift for the piano
few of her other pupils had.

When I touch the man
I love,
I want to thank my mother for giving me
piano lessons
all those years,
keeping the memory of Beethoven,
a deaf tortured man,
in mind;
  of the beauty that can come
from even an ugly
past.

WHAT I WANT IN A HUSBAND BESIDES A MUSTACHE

Well, to begin with,
you might as well not apply for the job
if you don't have
a mustache (

> or any plans
> for growing
> one
>)

and I tend to like men who are not too
tall,
say 5'8" or 9".
I like men with powerful shoulders
and prefer big hands;
no requirements for the size of your cock,
but you have to like to use it,
preferably just on—in me,
and be willing to fuck quite frequently
at least until we're 90.

That's another thing.
I want a man to be steady
To plan to be married to me
at least 50 or
60 years
with no sabbaticals.

I like men who read poetry,
and men who write turn me on even more (though I know that's
> trouble
In fact it's such a dangerous line that I think I'll reverse it:
men who write "don't turn me on")
if they're good.
I also only like ambitious men,

men who will take their destinies in their hands
and try to shape them.

I want a man who is mechanical,
physical,
likes to build,
work with his hands,
perhaps even a sportsman,
but one who does all these things with intelligence
and preferably learned them from
books.
I like a man who has faith in books.
That means he'll also have faith in me.
I'm a very long and imaginative book.

I'd also like my man to be a simultaneous traveler
and homebody,
one who would be happy working at home
with me,
or equally happy
out wandering around
looking at new things with me;
one who found himself the key to the meaning of the world,
and who found me the key to the meaning of himself.

I like a man
with good manners,
one willing to respond to the world;
a man who likes music,
and who has a definite style.

One who could earn a living,
though I'd contribute a good deal;
one who wanted a real woman
and who loved her

for her womanly
accomplishments.

A man who reads.
A man who likes painting.
A man who likes to talk in bed.
A man who likes the sun but thrives in the cold.
One who loves to touch my body.
Who kisses often.
Who types his letters.

One who drinks bourbon.
Who can ride a motorcycle.
Who collects books.
Who has a big dog.
Who calls my name in his sleep.

So far, I've only met one man like this;
but if you think you qualify,
write in for the application forms.
Truthfully,
you don't have much of a chance against
this first candidate.
But I'm democratic
and want to give everyone a chance.

Include a photo of your mustache.
I have not yet finished my document
describing the exact kinds of mustaches I prefer.
But that is an area of connoisseurship
to me.
Believe me,

there are some mustaches
that just wouldn't qualify.

I am known for my
discrimination.

INDIAN GIVER

You gave me
this knife
yesterday

an act
of friendship,
          because
I gave you
part of my lunch,
so you wouldn't have to eat
in the school cafeteria
and miss the ball game

Today you
take it
back.
     Indian giver,
I call you,
remembering I made a home run
yesterday at noon
and you
struck
out.

ANTICIPATION OF SHARKS

stay silent
keep away from sharks. stay
away from blood,
you will not be able to deal with a missing leg,
in the water/ you will bleed to death,
you will be the pain of a yard strewn with brown leaves,
and the shark will rake you clean,
strip your bones to their earth.

stay silent,
when you are in danger. The night is deep water.
The dark is a path of sharks,
their teeth flash
as the constellations,

The lonely night passes over me
as a submarine.
I am always lonely, will be
until I find someone to share my life with.
How lucky you are, good friend, to have taken up trout fishing.
I swim with sharks. They mistake me
for relatives.
We have nothing cold in common
but we glitter at each other.

And I stay silent,
as I swim in these waters,
more alone
than if I were by myself.

LETTERS TO SHEP

LETTER NUMBER ONE

23 February 1969
Dear Shep,
You lightning flash in my life, illuminating for a moment at least
everything,
this is a letter I can never send.
You are a man I may never see again in my life.
The tent you live in is soft,
touches my cheek
with sun
in winter.
You gave me nothing
except hope
and that is everything;

my life now
an iron sheet
a thick wooden lid
a heavy curtain

Rationality
gets one through life,
makes him a superior man (or woman),
allows him to meet the world on its own terms,
gives him many friends,
makes him live his life with commitment and honor
but it does not nourish him emotionally.
His wives leave him.
His lovers betray him.
He lives sanely and honestly
and the world heaves its irrational sighs
and bumps drunkenly against him.

43

I am a rational woman;
at the mercy of men who do not know how to love
but take what they want when they see it
and abandon it when it is inconvenient to hold,
heavy,

You could not carry me;
I was too heavy.
But I can't blame you;
no one else seems to be able to either.
I carry myself so well;
this pond makes me wonder
an image of a nature writer bashing frogs on the head, until there
were 40 of them dead, to make his supper;
where are you
anyone
when I need you?

Shep, you came closer to understanding than anyone.
How little like George Washington you are.
But you too live without knowledge of the desert.
I am the only one who can find water there,
lifting a leaf
I can find dew.
No one else sees it; this night/ this lonely night
It is my life.
my self-sufficient
lonely
life.

LETTER NUMBER TWO—AIRPLANE LETTER

Dear George Washington,
Between my dreams of broken airplane wings
and the city smoke that winds around my throat
like a scarf,
I sometimes think of you. Historical
broken airplane wing
from my own silver body;
smoke embedded in my lungs
from breathing
that cannot be removed.

a sphinx
sits on my tongue
and silently
speaks for me. I wanted to know
the answers:
reasons for planes crashing,
reasons for the wings crumbling off
and falling in mid-air,
reasons for the nose dives
we took in the night.

I sleep on plane trips
in order
not to be sick;
I do not look down,
scarcely even at the clouds like the heads of hundreds
of white-haired people sitting in church
beneath the plane;
I don't like the canned air
which smells of empty wastebaskets
and engine fatigue;
I dream even here

45

on this silvery airliner
of you
and your substitutes;
only words take my hand though.
And even they are faithless
and cannot mend the broken wings
of this plane I ride
through the warring smoky sky.

LETTER NUMBER THREE

Dear Shep,
Another letter I could not send,
from my empty life
like one of those caged hawks in a bird sanctuary
hearing all around me the other birds
small and thus free,
not rare and thus not so specially watched/

always I have been afflicted by my sense
of specialness,
and circumstance is something
I have tried and tried to explain;
why I was at a certain place at a certain time
and not somewhere else
when it would have been good.

I pull my body tighter into itself
daily. Find myself
tired with the burden of being alone.
Always I've been so isolated and empty,
even as a child,
standing still, so very still at the edge of
the purple hedge, waiting for butterflies

46

I could catch in my quiet 6-year-old
fingers, the dust of their wings
fatally rubbing off on my fingers. I wanted, longed for
beauty/ for music/ for love from beautiful people
And all I could find
were the butterflies no 6-year-old child
should have been so prematurely still to be able to
capture.
My feelings for you
escape when I am finding out about the world,
when I am working or performing or communicating with someone else; but each night,
every night
I am as lonely
as one tiger in a desert. One butterfly
in a jar.

How often do we meet people
we could love?
I do
about once every six months.
Usually
it is the wrong time
in their life. Sometimes
the wrong time
in mine.
The possibilities of imagination
are illusive.
If I can see a purple mountain
in the distance,
I can imagine everything on it/
but given a flat landscape
it is hard to imagine

for me, at least,
anything like a mountain
or what it might look like
there.

Seldom have women
with as much passion
or warmth
or ability to submit
willingly
been so alone
or so neglected
for so much of their lives. I am always
asking myself why
and then finding temporary solutions.

Sleep is a danger in my life,
offering me alternatives
that have nothing to do with it.
I am a good woman,
could cry sometimes for my
goodness/ would never take anything that I want
without honorable circumstances.
The poems in me right now
knot into my throat and become
birds
trying to get away.
This rib cage in me
presses against my enlarged heart
and I know the feeling of
those butterflies
I so desperately caught & trapped in jars
just to see to have
something beautiful
in my life.

THE MOON BEING THE NUMBER 19

to celebrate the centennial of the publication
of the Periodic Table of Elements, March 19,
1969

this year
they are looking for a new element.
Heavy.
Heavy enough to be dragging my heart down
now, as it hangs on the edges
of my veins.
I thought
all along
that it was the moon inside me
which made me so heavy.
                        I walked
          with its weight pressing
          on my brain,
               making me frown,
          and changing my vision,
                    pressing everything into hard
                    streaks
But the moon
is only a dead crust
that I've learned to lift
in each foot.
               It's this new element
that's been forming
in my blood
that tires me so.
                  And hurts me.

Potassium.
The number 19. I dreamed I was lying
         down

under a tree,
                    and 19 of your heavy faces
separately were shaven
by a Lithium beam. "Imagine,"
          I heard someone say,
"the moon wearing a
mustache.
              The moon is
a woman."
Potassium.
The number 19. I dreamed I was
              lying down
under a tree
              and 19 of your heavy hands
touched my face
heavily.
              And when I woke up, 19 of your
mustaches were lying
scattered
on the ground, and the
                    print
of your 20th hand
held me to the spot. This is absurd; how can
a hand, not there, hold me.
But that is the strange effect
of the missing element,
the heavy one
they are looking for.
                    It started its
formation
in my body
by disappointment. In other words
you wouldn't meet one. The riddle of calcium
              it becomes your teeth.
The riddle of potassium: it bathes me in blue light.

The riddle of the moon
and of the new heavy element
                              This sediment in my blood
that gives me poetry
and you nothing.

It is in my blood.
You refuse
the discovery.
                    You remember
                    another chemist.
And I ask you
if you ever properly memorized
your valences?
I don't catch
your answer,
having a heavy pressure now
on my ears
and not knowing where it will settle next
frightens,
              as I've never felt
frightened
              before.
                        You do not know how to love,
and you are afraid to
discover any new elements
in your life.
I,
the lover,
carry my heaviness inside me. Would not
recommend this as an easy way;
but the I Ching says

there is only one way
for the Superior Man.
     It is hard.
     It is heavy.
     It would frighten you
to even think about.
              Read Olson's Maximus Letter 12
and remember his tribute to the Tarot deck. Esoteric
          references?
Nothing is ever known
  until we autopsy
           the body.

Tonight
the sliver moon
hangs
to the edges
of my veins.

This awkward sky.

THE MOON HAS A COMPLICATED GEOGRAPHY

for Tony

The moon is murdered by
the movement
of the earth on its axis. Whatever exists
at night in my head
disappears in the daylight.

Same.
When I am with you
I'm a different person
than alone.

Was thinking
yesterday
how
for those of us who never live
except through
the people we love
life is never lived. It is always
somehow
an exercise for living it.
If we have any
moral or mental energy
life becomes a kind of procession
passing in front—
sometimes hidden behind—
us.
An object lesson
if we weigh
and analyze each event.
There is no life.

There is thinking
about
life.

For instance, yesterday I was waiting for the red light in order to cross the street. Several people stepped out though the light was red and crossed anyway, boldly. There were several cars coming which had to wait for them. Thinking the light was about to turn green and seeing that the cars were already stopped, I started out, off the curb, and was nearly run down by the first car which started up as soon as the jaywalkers were across

> An old man
> 60s
> grizzled face
> middle class
> in a Maroon Pontiac
> yelled angrily back at me,
> "You bastard,
> you stupid slob," as they
> speeded past.

By this time the light was green. I felt the usual twinge at a certain injustice. The people who had walked blatantly across on the red light and had held him up were not cursed. Only I who had waited till he stopped; till the light was changing.

"Only I"
that is the theme for object lessons
in the common life.
An unanswerable why.
Life lived as an object lesson
and not as life
fills you with terror
about the continual

juxtaposition of absurdity and
significance.

I am thinking about myself
now,
the moon,
the cup of milk,
the danger of walking without
anything but perception
thick glass lenses
that allow minutiae,
details of all the pounding each surface receives
details of the ugly real
surface.
Remember how the moon
that dead crust
lives
in reflected light
and of course
that it causes the tides
and madness
and flowers and beans grow fatter
under its fullness.
Moon,
is what I am thinking about.

Does anyone know my history
of meagerness?
My desert past?
My empty cupboard life?
My drained memory cells?
How light my gravity is?
How I give away everything
I have
fearing for it

55

that it might dry up
with me?
The moon is not moist and cool,
it is a hot breath of air
rattling through the
parched leaves
on a dusty day
a pair of cracked lips
against a burning forehead.
How our lives are filled with paradox.

Those who most need love
are the unlovable.

I cannot talk to strangers,
and I have no friends;
I sleep with the light on
all night
when I am alone.
When you leave me for a few days
the salt disappears
from my body.

I ask for your love
and I have nothing to offer
but my own in return.
What is that?
Not moonlight
but the invisible dry moon
with a complicated
geography.

I heard
from your friend
about you. That you woke up

in the woods
with a fox
statue-like
looking at you from the tent flap.
You did not wake up in
the night,
I'm sure
though the moon certainly
was around
nudging the fox
moving under the leaves
in the bleached white
swollen buried seeds preparing to
emerge from the ground.
That is the way of the world.
We hear
about those we love
from strangers.
Who is to say what love is
except those who feel it?
There is a common problem we share:
everyone loves,
few are loved.
Where does it go? This moisture,
the coolness,
the motions of loving?
The night you come home to me
the moon will be full
and someone else's madness
will start.

FOR A (1) COLD, (2) HARD, (3) MEAN, (4) NASTY, (5) NONE OF THESE SCULPTOR I LIKE

I am the daydreamer
with a sliver of moon absently caught under
my silver foot;
I shut myself away
in a room where the doors are wired to your fingers

you would
be jolted
if you ever saw
my dreams.
My eyes
are promises
of steel rods lancing your body
or broken glass
strewn in my mouth
torturous and bloody before you ever even
touch
my lips. Every word
seduces you
away from me.
            like a journeying tiger
            changing mountains
            in Tibet
My woman's voice
& soft hands
remind you of the women
you almost love.
of your own loneliness, & most of all
the years that pass
eaten up by machines
            power hammers
            and visions of hot Bethlehem steel

a furnace in your heart
no woman could ever endure
the temperatures of.

You remind me
with your strong body,
Polish face,
and deep laugh
of my father
the man who rejected me and left me
when I was 2.

I look at you with a kind of
2-year-old longing
consequently.

I am one of those poor art students
you spoke of,
banging
pounding on your door
at 5 a.m.

Winter branches
shadow my face. It is
a door,
a deep dream,
a secret room,
holding back all my soft
womanly words.

Love,
I ask myself,
what is that?
Something you lost sight of when you were 2
and the last sight of your father's

white uniform hat
bobbed
down the driveway and
disappeared?

You, cautious man,
you, whom I lie here in bed
looking out at my winter landscape and dreaming of,
you welder
burning into my steel dreams,
you can
not know
how much more cautious and frightened and angry
I am
      even, than you,
I,
the daydreamer,
with razor blades behind my smile.

Don't frighten me
or you'll upset the acid
from the shelf on the roof of my mouth.

You are a man
I could love.
I only find them
every 6 months
or so.
That means I will run
run frantically
when I see you.
I want to cry
I want to scream
I want to swear or laugh
all very loud

to let out the anger
the hurt
the pain
that you remind me of. But I've only
closed my door,
gone behind the branches of the trees
—the place where some moons
hide
at night.

I LAY NEXT TO YOU ALL NIGHT, TRYING AWAKE TO UNDERSTAND THE WATERING PLACES OF THE MOON

I lay next to you
all night,
trying,
awake,
to understand the watering places
of the moon,
        how my own body
dry and restless
like rootless tumbleweed
moves through the night,
through my eyes,
staying awake in bed
while you sleep
allowing my presence
but not wanting to touch,
allowing my presence
in the way
the earth
tolerates the moon,
allowing its restless pull.

I lay next to you
all night,
trying,
awake,
to understand what dead moon
I am,
why I shine in the sky at all.

But it is a physical function
of presence.

The moon
never complains.
The moon knows
it shines
at night
moving relentlessly
awake
through the sky
while everyone else sleeps,
while you're away.
                    The metaphor fatigues me.
I am less patient from my sleepless night.
I could carry the moon
across this room,
across the lawn,
out through the wet morning streets
through this whole town
and make
references
that would make you
as impatient with my life
as I am.

           But my sharp tongue
gleams at me
out of its drawer,
a sharpened knife,
and reminds me of the people I've been chiding
for the past few weeks,
telling them to burn
like the sun,
telling them to ignore the lack of love in their lives,
telling them to smile and walk past telescopes
photographing their dissatisfactions
like craters on the moon,

telling them to name them and find
new landscapes,
while I lie awake
next to you
all night
trying
to understand why
the sun's rays leave me so hot and thirsty,
why I am lonely and chilly at night,
why I,
the avid astronomer,
allow myself to be confused
and look out of the wrong end of the telescope.

Forgive me
for my restlessness
and my expectations.
I am the moon. Diane.
Poets have speculated about me too long.
At last I am circled,
photographed,
and soon to be explored.
A dry dusty shell
of something that once lived.
My literary content
is a vanishing species,
like sea otters.
Forgive me if I dive into the desert every night
and call out for water.
Forgive me if I dive into the moon, myself,
and cannot escape the pull of your gravity.
Forgive me if I expect you to love me. I mistake you
for a poet.
I lay next to you
all night,

trying,
awake,
to understand the watering places
of the moon,
knowing there are no Li Pos left
to drunkenly fall into a river
attempting to hold its radiant face
all night.
My dry arms
try to gather
water.

NO MORE SOFT TALK

Don't ask a geologist about rocks.
Ask me.

That man,
he said.

What can you do with him?
About him?
He's a rock.

No, not a rock,
I said.
     Well,
a very brittle rock, then.
One that crumbles easily, then.
Is crushed to dust, finally.

Me,
I said.
I am the rock.
The hard rock.
You can't break me.

I am trying to think how a woman
can be a rock,
when all she wants is to be soft,
to melt to the lines
her man draws for her.

But talking about rocks
intelligently
must be

talking about different kinds
of rock.

What happens to the brain
in shock? Is it
like an explosion
of flowers and blood,
staining the inside
of the skull?

I went to my house,
to see my man,
found the door locked,
and something I didn't plan
on—a closed bedroom door
(my bed),
another woman's handbag on the couch.
Is someone in the bedroom?

Yes, yes,
a bed full of snakes all bearing new young,
a bed full of slashed wrists,
a bed of carbines and rifles with no ammunition,
a bed of my teeth in another woman's fingers.

Then the answer to rocks,
as I sit here and talk.

The image of an explosion:
a volcanic mountain
on a deserted Pacific island.
What comes up,
like gall in my throat,
a river of abandoned tonsils that can no longer cry,

a sea of gold wedding rings and smashed glasses,
the lava, the crushed and melted rock
comes pouring out now,
down this mountain you've never seen,
from this face that believed in you,
rocks that have turned soft,
but now are bubbling out of the lips of a mountain,
into the ocean, raising the temperature
to 120 degrees.
If your ship were here
it would melt all the caulking.

This lava,
hot and soft,
will cool someday,
and turn back into the various stones.
None of it is
my rock.
My rock doesn't crumble.

My rock is the mountain.
Love me
if you can.
I will not make it easy for you
any more.

THE EQUINOX

for Tony

March 19.

This day, like any
other, is a bullet shot from your rifle,
passage unnoticed
unless something spectacular was caught.
But who counts the shells
after they're gone? And says,
        "Where did this one go,
                and this?"
Who lies awake nights
trying to remember where every single shot
was fired? Or days?
                What happened to
                every one?

Still, this day
approaches abstraction. The day when the sun rose at 6:05 a.m.
and the sun set at 6:05 p.m.
The day of equality
                and that is an idea,
                an abstraction.
The equinox,
        a term used to express
        either the moment at which
        or the point at which
        the sun apparently crosses
        the celestial equator . . . compliments Encyclopaedia
                                Britannica.

Equality. Something which none of us has.
Few can equal your mechanical skills
or your strength,
even your unpracticed markmanship.

"Apparently," says the book, meaning it's the way we look at it
that describes the sun crossing the equator of Celeste
            imagine her long sequined dress
            spangling her hips, the sun,
            an Ethiopian diplomat in a dinner jacket
            embroidered with ivory buzzards,
            crimson branches holding them,
            crosses her face and marceled hair with a hand
            heavy in signet rings
But March 19 is your birthday
and there is nothing apparent about you. Or everything.
You are what you appear to be; and not.
More and less
sometimes, as we all are
sometimes
and so
on.

To continue with the book,
        At the time
        of the equinox
        it is commonly believed that
        strong gales may be expected.

Well, there could never be gales of laughter in March.
The grass is sodden, and too much rain gets into
the cracks everywhere.

I never expect a gale when I am with you.
Your presence

70

on the contrary
is like a silencer on a gun.
(and please do not neglect all the implications
of my metaphor. The trouble with comparing a poet
to a gun is that poets are not used deliberately
to kill with, and send my compliments to Jack Spicer
wherever he is . . .)

and the book again,
      This popular idea has
      no foundation in fact,
      for continued observations
      have failed to show any unusual prevalence
      of gales at this season.

On the eve of the equinox
I discharge these March 19th greetings to you
      may gales of love in the form of short-black-skirted
      young waitresses from your favorite restaurant in Kansas
      City regale you with whatever you desire,
      and may the gales of love that could not be found elsewhere
      at this season be found rippling the ends of your mustache,
      may all the lofts in Manhattan need plumbing,
      and may all the sons be equal and share spangled Celeste,
      whenever she crosses your street on the arm of
      her Ethiopian diplomat,
      may every March 19th not be a shot in the dark
      for you
            let us remember your mother
      had a very good aim
      giving her son a chance to cross the celestial equator
      this time
      around.

FILM: CALLED 5 BLIND MEN

The poet is not
the blind man/ rather
he writes
for the man
who cannot see,
                            making
moving pictures
vivid as walking through a room,
the floor covered with
animate snakes
—some yellow or brown, black,
   a green mamba, corals,
   diamondbacks/
some huge and fat,
others shining, skinny,
short, long—all moving
and looking at him
with flat triangular noses
& fast eyes,
                    Where does he put his foot?

Here is a still from the movie:
black and white film,
showing 5 men standing against a leafless woods.
I am the heroine
of the movie. You never see me,
but I tell you
who these men are,
and in what ways I love them all. I look back
in the film,
on my life with them.
They are all mountain climbers. And that's when
this photo was taken—when they were together

planning an expedition to
Canada.
The photo is one that I, you, the audience,
can find in an old drawer
and remember from 40 years ago, these men now
old or dead, or listed & described in biographies
as their friends
(like old Hemingway photos).

From left to right, they are
Julian Harmony, stocky, muscular, straight dark hair,
a bristly mustache, always tan from fishing,
wearing a white shirt open down the front of his hairy chest,
sleeves rolled up, the most
articulated face of the five,
with its dark shadows
making you feel he could drink a quart of bourbon
at one sitting and still be telling
good stories;
David Garrison, the handsome one,
the one I have to confess I fall in love with,
standing in front of the tree trunk,
light hitting him as if he should be the hero of anyone's life,
the only one looking elegant, like a man of the boulevards,
in a light tweed suit, high vest,
sideburns,
his nose flat, obviously having been broken once
but skillfully reset,
a wool tie and you feel there must be,
though not seen in the photo,
a heavy gold watch chain;
Gordon Quails is the center figure,
a brash smile over his turtle-neck sweater,
wide forehead; looks Irish,
friendly, has both arms draped around his friends

(the only man who touches the others),
you can see him in pubs on afternoons,
laughing and telling stories at everybody's expense;
the fourth man
has a fleshy face and a pointed nose like a woodpecker,
round, metal-rimmed glasses,
bangs, a shy smile, doesn't look into
the camera. He is Carl Scandor, he writes poetry
and can name all the plants which grow above
an altitude of 5,000 feet. He looks like
he thinks about god;
at the far right of the photo is the 5th man,
O. K. Ready. His initials stand for
Oscar Karl, but his friends cannot resist calling him O. K.
He's the tallest man of the 5
and is big and bear-like. He wears an undershirt
with long loose sleeves and looks like he's secretly
planning some very devious tricks.
His face has the expression a hawk might have
as it circles over a grain field and sees a
rippling pattern that means a small mammal
is moving through it, ready, if he's fast enough, to be grabbed.

You must use
your imagination
for this film. It is in 5 parts,
each part
a love poem
to one of the five blind men.

I Love Song to Julian Harmony

> "And if my sister hadn't died in an auto wreck
> & had been taken by the injuns
> I would have something to do:
> go into the mountains & get her back."
>
> Jim Harrison

a hunting we shall go,
for the extinct white wolf & the illegal doe,
her belly swollen, containing your sister/
a story the Indians tell
of a lonely white man—he was the moon,
his cock stiff, pushing open our eyes,
full of light to shine in the dark woods,
in a smothering of brown leaves,
coupling, with a deer,
fucking her, mounting her,
as she moved on delicate hooves, her feet
were the wind that left silver prints,
her eyes were broken branches.

I am stolen
from the grass where I sleep
this warm afternoon,
waking up to a shadow standing over me. I think
for a minute
it is an eagle;
but it's you,
throwing stories over me like fish nets filled with stars
and your mustache hypnotizes the sun,
preventing it from setting/ we are
flooded with day,
your hands are strong enough to push
night away.
You will rescue me;
it is something to do/ to let you
call yourself a man.

II Love Poem for David Garrison

> "The sign said SWIM AT YOUR OWN RISK
> and I did
> but everything I've ever done
> has been at my own risk."
>
> Dan Gerber

You told me
you raced cars
until you broke all your ribs,
both your legs,
both arms,
cut up your face
& broke your nose.

I

wonder
why
you do not look
broken
or cut
but stand
liltingly
ready to rescue me
from my contract with General Motors.
My feet are swans
that screech at the ground I must walk;
my hands are angry weasels
that crush the necks of chickens;
my face is a bad-tempered carnivore,
a Bengal tiger,
and I only fall in love with men who wear mustaches;
so drive me in your Ferrari
along the boulevards of Paris
and try to win me over
with your clean-shaven face. You
are the one

76

who's the most adventurous. You only like things
where you must
take a risk;
but inside my mouth, reaching down into my throat,
like a doctor trying to take out my tonsils,
is a sign that says LETHAL.
And we are riding in this car on the boulevards.
Even without a mustache,
you look
so elegant. I have died in an auto wreck.

III Love Song for Gordon Quails

> "I'll never write a love poem
> so long as there are white plains
> in the place of love."
> George Quasha

In this life
I will be a pianist.
I will not have shaky hands.
I will give concerts of Beethoven & Chopin
until I come to a bird sanctuary in the white woods of Michigan
and then I'll marry the man I love;
each stroke of my strong fingers,
golf clubs wielded by handsome, mustached, gray-haired
                                    gentlemen,
will add one note at a time to a piece of music
that will make the world
turn out all its lights.
I will scatter morning-glories
around the feet of the man I love. Their trumpets
will be filled with snow from
the woods,
and love will replace words.

You come stamping into the bar,

77

sit by the fire, drinking ale. Your cheek is icy,
cool, as I come and sit on your lap,
putting my face next to yours.
My tongue has been cut out.
This is something I've always feared. But
I no longer
suffer from it.
With love,
with steady hands and a keyboard to embrace,
words are unnecessary,
and a love song
is your arm around me,
your cold face.
Chords that take ten fingers to play.

IV Love Song to Carl Scandor

> "I say to the lead
> why did you let yourself
> be cast into a bullet?"
>
> Charles Simic

There is a wooden church on the hill.
It is empty of everything but a woodpecker.
There is a girl here who complains.
She has a bullet in her foot.
She dreams of motorcycles at night.
There is no altar in this church.
She dreams the church service is conducted by ten
angels riding Harley-Davidsons.
They are not the seraphim
or cherubim.
They all have mustaches
and
they ask her
one question

from the pulpit:
     Will you follow us to heaven?
She comes in with wild flowers
squashed into the mud
on the sole of her shoe.
She answers all questions,
"Yes."
She loves her god.
She asks him why he's given
her this difficult face.
His angels
even
cannot answer her question.

V Love Song for O. K. Ready

> "Each man who dances
> with the bride must
> pin a dollar to her dress"
>
> "gnawed foot in a trap"
>   J. D. Reed

My heart
was caught
in a trap
15 years ago. I have not
like a wise animal
been able to gnaw it off
and run away.
                    To cut out the heart
is to—
this is obvious—
cut out life.

What do you go hunting for?
What guns do you use?

79

What kind of bullets?
Would you rather die from a gun or an auto wreck?
Would you ever resort to traps?

I am a not-very-blond Polack.
I've never been to a Polish wedding.
I've never had dollars pinned to my dress.
I have tried to gnaw out my heart.
Dance with me.
My dress is blood-soaked
and stiff from trying to bite out of the trap.

Where there is love
there is pain.
When I leave your house
I will have to leave
a little blood behind—a footprint on the doorstep.

Forgive me.
.   .   .
All the men I've loved
are blind.
They do not see how tightly you must hold
a woman
who loves you; she will
slip out of your hands
like a strong fish.

When I walk into a room
I see all the men
as potential lovers. I spend my life
writing poems.
Men pass me
like traffic on a six-lane highway.
The men I love

don't even look at me
as they drive by.
They are as blind to my fears
as to my love.
The woman
is the camera, then;
the eye
of the world.

TO THE CHAMP OF PINBALL MACHINE BASEBALL

The knuckler
is a pitch
nobody can hit; so I've learned
not to push the button
that tosses it.

Who
ever
heard
of
a steel baseball
but stealing my bases,
"You've knocked me off
my pins," I could say.

Really
there is no way
to pin us
down.
"That's the ball game," or
"You won't get to first base,"
they say
but I've never
liked
games.
A ball
is a different
matter
however.

"Knuckle down to work,"
they say
but this knuckler

goes so far
afield
I lose my
balance
trying to take
your pitch.

A sportsman
may
tape his wrists
but you kiss mine,
and I squeeze your hand
making the knuckles white
down white;
white as a new softball. White as
the inside of my hand
or the other parts of me
you will probably never touch.

· · · · · · · ·

FIVE LOVE POEMS

· · · · · · · ·

WORK

I always write
my love letters/ white pumas
that jump on my shoulders
and bite my cheek

GREEN TONGUE

When I meet the man I love
I am speechless
Unripe apples adhere to the green branches
They make smart-ass comments when people try to pick them.
Loose & ripe, they fall/ maybe you hear a thud
when they hit the ground.

LOVE POEM

My stripes
make me
a tiger. Definitions
are not always
so easy.

TELEGRAM

Your hand
was a lie.

LOVE NOTE

The white flesh
of an apple
falls out of my heart
untouched by
                pumping blood

SUNFLOWERS IN MY WRIST

When I wake up
I see how empty
the room is.
                    Sunlight
like a cold beer
                    coming into the room.

The possibilities
of day
occur to me.
But the chances of your being part of the day
are smaller than a sunflower
growing in my hotel room.

Good morning,
I say,
to myself
and that slick
sunshine.
                    It slides through my hair
                    making me an image
                    animated
                    but lifeless
                    on the screen of your eye.
The seeds
of the sunflowers
pitting against my breasts
my face
as I wake up
with pains in my wrists this morning.
Seeds
of the sunflower

When I wake up
tangled in my own legs
& hair
having dreamed you put your hands on all
those chunks of amber
lumping up my breasts & throat,
those poems
I cannot get out of me

        those words
              that lie coiled up
                     at the foot of my bed
      under the sheets
             hidden in the covers
                  waiting
      I fear
      to uncoil
      like mean black snakes
      & slither over me
             into my mouth
                at night

THE CATALOGUE OF CHARMS

a surrealist poem for that
charming Ray Matela

Charming.
You are charming as snakes and the half-moon
in an ancient piece of jewelry;
you are
charming as swift lizards and the blazing sun
carved in the handle of a Portuguese dagger;
you are
charming as a golden whippet biting the handle of a mirror;
charming is the word/
a shooting star,
fire that stiffens out alone in a dark night.

                              And I
waiting for a charming man,
one with a mustache lurking over his mouth
who is waiting to touch my belly, my hips,
                with lizards,
                with half-moons cutting off my breath like metal
                collars,
                exciting me
                with deadly white empire snakes
                inching along my shoulders
                eying me like daggers of the sun,
                shivering through my thighs,
                mirrors doubling, tripling, quadrupling the golden
                dogs that race from my outstretched feet,
oh, charming
I find you,
touching my face with your eyes,

90

no, it's charm
that brandishes heavy swords at me.
                              Says
beware
of that charming man with the mustache
who turns you on.
Keep him at arm's length,
keep him a day away,
keep him farther than the handle of the rake,
                                        he is
charming,
          so,
                be sure
                      that you
keep him like fire
beyond the tips of your fingers,
keep him a car's length ahead of you
keep him in your rear-view mirror,
don't let him tail-
gate you.
                Your shadow dogs you.
The sun makes it.
The crescent moon mimics it. You are alone,
a ray from the sun,
deadly, ultraviolet rays, lilac in hue, you
deadly Portuguese man o' war,
you sting ray,
you ray gun. Charming,
you charm me with rays of moonlight,
man-rays, a charming portrait
painter, I beware,
you know,
of artists
who are too charming.

Only I
am allowed
to be deadly
with charm
with fire dancing around my eyes,
smudging them,
daring them to pass you on the street,
remembering your charm,
                        the night
that races along my breasts like greyhounds
like whippets carved out of gold
and biting my fingers.
In my ears are mirrors
reflecting all the rays of light
from moon or sun.
Charming,
you are
charming as the rock-crystal eye of the bull,
as chalcedony representations of my heart
which must be hard and rocky.

                        Your charm
is something I must keep,
like the horizon,
always in the distance,
like a ray of light
                —insubstantial,
except as a source of power,
as an illumination,
as something which cannot be held
or possessed.

THE LAMENT OF THE LADY BANK DICK

dedicated to Fay Dunaway and
the discoverers of Tanzanite,
with a little sigh for W. C. Fields

I ruffle the pages of the Sahara Desert
burnishing the lips of old movie stars and remind myself
of a dual existence.
                    You
the gangster I am trying to reform, your
long mustaches dripping down from your jaw, tangling
into dreams of Garands,
as you sit
in Max's Kansas City,
the bar
all operators know about. I, the lady bank dick
threatening your masculine role
with the .22 pistol
I always carry hidden
in a place only you'd
think to look.
                    And our involvement is an historical one
(though I laugh that our entanglement came in 1969),
because what you run away from
is not Alcatraz or San Quentin,
but me.
I am small and soft and elegant. A woman
law-abiding men dream of,
slipping into their lives;
wearing my trench coat; sliding through long countries
in my Maserati;
driving them away from bank payments and wives,
shadowing my eyes with their honest hands. But how can I
love these straight men?

I tail the one I love,
the man who's taken millions from the Chemical Trust.
                    (Don't
                    they say,
                    "When a woman's needs are financial,
                    her reaction is chemical"?)
Yes, you are my hero. More than that.
It's my job to trace you, tripping past your heavy footprints,
knowing they are a ruse,
to place my eyelashes heavily against your ear
and whisper into your bourbon.
You are the completely contemporary criminal,
dreaming of past masters.
You have to be called
Tony "The Head" Tanzanite—
a new jewel,
imitating Legs Diamond.
You, turned on to some trip in Africa where I also hunt
for another prize,
an embezzler. Underneath my trench coat
I am nothing but a little ten-foot sloop,
my sail handmade,
whipping me along.
                    Is it Harry Winston or Mr. Tiffany
who is paying me to track you down,
Mr. Tanzanite? Banks are your real hangout,
but one jewel robbery hangs around your neck
like stop and go signals.
You try to drop the rocks into your bourbon at Max's Kansas City,
but the waitresses return them,
say, "Oh, you've forgotten this." You only want
to get away,
you say,
to another country.

You want to carry your stolen cash with you
and make a real life, but this one you've started has
defined you a criminal
and you have to hang out where you're loved
for being one. Your cronies at the bar
have stakes in making you love your life and reputation.
And you are even a little intrigued by me,
small with wrists threaded with iron,
following you in my trench coat and fast car.
                                        You like

the idea of the woman
who's the dick,
the one with all the strength behind her eyelashes.
                                        You've used yours

up in all those robberies.
Your mustaches betray you. And your cold eyes that
fight with the ice cubes and stolen Tanzanite.

Our fascinations
have to contradict, of course,
our cultural roles. You must kill me—for I'm the cop
and you're the robber. Whether to preserve your identity
as thief par excellence or to escape to another
land.
Another country.
Another life.
I must be destroyed because my role serves me
as the woman who chases you,
who would remind you of the past,
of your weaknesses,
and who would ask you to change the future.

My heart is not in my role.
It drops between my legs.
It beats in my cunt,

95

like sun strokes.
I seduce all these con men,
these gangsters,
these robbers & embezzlers, I chase.
My heart is in my work,
I tell my employers.
And they buy gas for my Maserati,
spend hundreds on my expense account that includes
Belgian lace, thin silk, and French perfume.
But they dream of me
as a good dick, and confuse my role.
They do not notice my heart
being battered and crushed with each job.

I fall in love with you,
the man I must pursue.
Your face is wanted.
And I would not ever have had any success
if I were not
willing to fuck the world,
throw aside every expectation, every role;
if I were not willing to die
any time,
a hundred machine-gun holes lacing me,
proving my womanly parts.
                    Contra-"dick"-ting my title.
My final act would be to throw
all my guns
in your lap.
But I am a woman
who has chosen a glamorous role,
one that puts her on a slippery footing with adventurous men.
To die would be easier than
to deny this role.
I would not have met you,

Mr. Tanzanite,
had you not been a dreamy thief
by definition. To lament the end of my life now
would be to deny
the inevitable.
But I do lament it. Being a woman.
And underneath,
still, so very soft.

Introduction to "The Ten-Dollar Cab Ride." I heard Robert Duncan tell a story about himself many years ago when his life seemed more hopeless to him than it does now. The problems of not having enough money, of feeling that the world inadequately appreciated his work, made him think of taking his own life. Like most people who consider killing themselves, he didn't want to do it right that minute. Apparently he had ten dollars in his pocket—all the money he had—and he decided that he would take a cab ride and when the ten dollars was used up on the meter, get out and kill himself.

However, he made the mistake of choosing Golden Gate Park—a very beautiful place—for his cab ride. And when $10 registered on the meter, he felt so good that he had to get out and walk home.

In the summer of 1969, when the astronauts were landing on the moon, I was having some of those same feelings about my own life. And I also felt a strange kind of dubiousness about their landing on the moon, an image which, as a poet and as a person named after the moon, I had begun to think of as my own property.

THE TEN-DOLLAR CAB RIDE

for Robert Duncan

Robert,
>like the spray from a waterfall,
>I am white,
>like snow blindness,
>like the belly of a shark,
>like sweet white peaches
>or the inside of a Pinot Chardonnay grape,
>bone china,
>zinc-white pigment,
>or the contrast of a mechanic's white back
>with his grease-soaked arms,
>I am
>the moon.
>>My name,
>Diane,
>>giving you a glance at a white ankle,

a pale wrist,
shadowed by bracelets.

I am something
no one has ever touched,
a place no one has ever landed,
reputedly covered with powdery volcanic dust
which might explode when exposed to oxygen,
something dreamt of,
a place to put a flag,
something to conquer,
white dust to step carefully, artistically on
where you hope
>no one has ever stepped
>before.

You told, Robert,
Robber Baron of moonlit nights,
of your taxi ride
one pale moment
into Golden Gate Park.
                    $10 you had
in your pocket.
                    You could have had a pocket
                    of wolfbane, of gold codpieces, of a
                    pair of peacock-blue stockings worn by H. D.,
                    or old lines from the poet Pindar,
                    you could have had mesmerized butterflies
                    in your pocket, or crystalized bumblebees,
                    the fork of an adder's tongue,
                    the wishbone of a partridge,
                    or a cap that made you invisible.

Instead, poet,
you had
$10
and your life was like mine is
right now.
                    You had no one to possess you,
                    no one who wanted you,
                    to give you one of the chambers of his heart
                    to sleep in.
No one owns the moon,
                    yet,
                        you know.
And so you decided you would
ride
as far as your $10
would take you.
Then you'd get out of the car and blow out your brains.

100

I have been riding this particular taxi
for 30 years.
   Old moon,
   Young moon,
   I don't even know what I am
      any more.
Like you,
I am unprepared to give up,
to step out of the cab and die,
the meter by now
registers up in the millions.
I cannot afford to get out and pay. Must keep riding. Lucky man,
you got out when the clock said
$10
and walked home.
     But I am the moon
Where can I go?

Everyone wants to conquer me,
to use me,
to put a missile base on me,
to extract my ore,
to bounce radio waves off me.

Now there is something faintly humorous
about all this
moon-june campy sentiment.
I wish I were Yeats and could abandon poetry.

Then I'd invoke myself,
     Diane,
      the moon,
        make love to myself,
forget about the sun's rays that light me up every day.

101

forget about who the moon has been
take heart
            (another poet's word)
that soon
I'll be American territory,
throw away my old face &
name
Someday,
            get in a taxi,
            and say to the driver,
            "Take me to the moon."
            And laughing
            we would drive away.

The charge, of course,
at the end of the ride
would be $10.

(and I would get a discount for having written this poem,
taken this trip.)

WITH WORDS

for Tony

Poems come from incomplete knowledge.
From the sense of seeing
an unfinished steel bridge
that you'd like to walk across,
your imaginary footprints floating like pieces
of paper,
where the metal ends,
on the cold water
far below;
or the moon disappearing
behind a cloud
just when you could almost
see the face
of the man standing next
to you
in the olive trees;

And consequently,
I write about those
whose hands
I've touched once,
trying to remember
which fingers had the rings
on them,
speculating from a few words
what the dialogue of a lifetime
would have been,
making the facts up
out of the clouds of breath we release
on a winter night.

How can I
then
make a poem for you?
whose skillful hands
could make expert
blueprints
of all my bones?
There is no need
for a bridge between us;
we sleep on the same side of the bed.
Your mustache.
inherited from some stealthy Cossack
who kissed your great-great-great-
grandmother
and slid his icy cock between her warm
legs one night
is no mystery
to me.
I can relive
its history,
drawing lines all over my body.
I have no questions
either
about your powerful legs,
arms,
back,
or the quick mind
which leads the body around on a leash.

Forgive me then,
if the poems I write
are about the fragments,
the broken bridges,
and unlit fences
in my life.

104

For the poet,
the poem
is not
the measure
of his love. It is
the measure
of all he's lost, or
never seen,
or what has no life,
unless he gives it life
with words.

The only man who's never
betrayed me
is my accountant.

CITIZEN'S TRUST

The moon is something
you can trust.
The sun is someone else we
all trust,
that banker at his window every morning
behind bars.

Now I've moved
like bees
into your hair

POEM TO A MAN WITH GOOD TASTE

I was abandoned
for a Norton Matchless.

BLACK LEATHER BECAUSE BUMBLEBEES LOOK LIKE IT

when the bumblebees ride their black motorcycles down to the
country to watch death swimming in the river, nude,
enjoying the summer, and me, gathering mushrooms in the shade
nearby,
everything is quiet and peaceful.
Death and I get along because we are not too personal.
And my life is like Chinese to him; he doesn't read it or understand.
But his black clothes and leather cap
thrown on the bank carelessly
remind me of my children, like hundreds of bee carcasses, tossed
together
and dead from a storm that wrecked the hive.
Watch him,
death,
climb out of the river, without his clothes.
Isn't he beautiful? A man built to swim and ride.
Shall we swim together, Mr. Big Beautiful, and Black Death?
Push over the rocks,
gather watercress, and smile at the fish?
Isn't it nice in the country, Mr. Death?
If I put a frame around your clothes, lying on the bank,
so that just in the corner of the picture, we might see one
of your bare feet climbing out of the water—
death's foot,
and the bees nearby, and me lying nude on the bank while the bees
ride by—
what would you think of that, Mr. Death?
Would you still think my name Chinese?
And would we still get along?
Oh, Mr. Death, I've seen you so many times.
How is it we meet so often, yet never speak?

TO CELEBRATE MY BODY

where
you had only
to touch me
others had
to present a history,
a bibliography,
and a justification

but

no question
remains,
that a gift
easily given
lightly received
is wasted

no one can
touch me
the way
you can/ I should say
did

but

no question
remains
your touch
was not lightly
taken

and
my body

108

has spent
a lot of years
awakening

too long
in fact
to stop
the process

your touch
is
somewhere across
the ocean. My imagination
has never
been poor; but
cannot extend
to a life
where touching
comes only
in a letter

Celebrate
the word.
we
are both
poets;
taking the world
ultimately
seriously

but the word
can only
give life
if it acknowledges

the lips
the mouth that made it

the body
that pumped the
sounding air

where
you had only
to touch me
others had
to present a history
a bibliography
a justification

the touch
comes first
remains
is the last thing you
remember
after you
turn
out
the light
at night.

THE MECHANIC

to T.W.

Most men use
their eyes
like metronomes
clicking off the beats
of a woman's walk;
how her hips press
against the cloth, as figs just before
they split their purple skins
on the tree,
measuring how much of her walk
goes into bed at night,
the jar of the sky
being filled with the Milky Way
glittering for every time
she moves her lips

but of course
the secrets
are not the obvious beats
in the song
that even a bad drummer can play

hearing the speed of the motor
—it too made up of beats—
so fast,
subtle, I suppose,
they register
as continuous sound
or the heart which of course
beats without any fan belt to keep it
cool,

it is a test,
a rhythm,
they could not see
with those measuring eyes
though perhaps there are some
whose fingers and ears
are so close to the motors
with clean oil passing through their ears
and draining properly into the brain pan,
perhaps a few . . .

who can tell
what the secret bleeding of a woman
is all about

As a woman
with oily stars sticking
on all the tip points
of my skin
I could never
trust a man
who wasn't a mechanic,
a man who uses his
eyes,
his hands,
listens to
the
heart.

TO THE WIVES

You beautiful neat women
who always sleep between clean sheets
and have the comfort of children at your dinner tables,
fearing me,
the maverick stranger with flying hair
and bohemian ways,
as I talk to your husbands about poetry——my life——
because the poem is my green wind,
the song that winds me into a mountain of thick stones.
You have less to fear from me
than from your own friends. I would not steal
your husbands
——even if I could——
I would not even sleep with them or flirt in the back rooms . . .
I am a woman,
one with an urge to know, to move, to
understand.
I sing, I talk, I make love to
the mountains,
but I would not betray you,
though I envy you.
To do so
would be to betray my own future.
I, who constantly talk of honesty and wholeness and the hard but
good way of life——commitment——
do you think I would reinforce anyone's false dream of freedom?
Freedom
is in your head. It is a dark room
that frightens and haunts us all
from our days as children. Somehow, we,
the women,
who have often been kept inside to care for children,
or have tried to serve the lives of men not our equals,

113

we have learned, and know, should know,
how necessary it is to find freedom, in the kitchen, in the
cell, in the bedroom, in our own hands, wherever we may be.
We do not have the world afflicting us,
besetting us with complicated bargains
and unreal expectations.
We should have learned better to control our desires,
to live for the beauty,
that fire that burns so bright,
our reality.
                    And I chide you
sweet wives
for not knowing me better, not seeing what an ally you have in
me, for proving inadvertently what your husbands have been saying,
that women cannot think or reason or perceive,
that they are deceitful and don't understand honor.

Yes, I am often a woman alone.
Yes, I like men, love them even,
wait for the one who might ever be my equal,
my partner;
Yes, I ache when I have to sleep alone at night
as I often do,
when my sun god, my King of Spain is not with me,
but I am enough of a woman to know
I would not be happy
with another woman's husband
even for a night,
that I would anguish for the woman I want to be.

I do not want to possess anything. Or to be possessed;
Yes, I need the illusion of both in my life,
don't we all?
Please,
you beautiful soft faces,

114

even you not so beautiful, hardened hurt women,
who are wives,
understand me. Listen to me. A man can talk to me for 10 minutes
and understand my reality,
my humanity,
how much I like the world, myself, and him;
I don't have to fuck him
to prove it. Please
you are always asking for equal rights. I plead now
that you pay with equal understanding.
Have compassion for men,
for me;
for our lonely lives.
I am not sleeping with your men. I am only reading to them
—how I love them,
how I need them to listen—
my poems, as I now read/talk to you.
My poems, the snails on the wet garden path,
the small parts that make a motorcycle run.

CAVES

You spelunker,
you talented, charming, smart,
well-educated girl from
a good family,
you argument against my will to live,
you reminder of my own defective genes,
of my cavernous head with gothic columns of longing,
do you really want to map me,
to know why I am who I am,
what has created these walls of twisting
gnarled salty stone,
why water has served as acid
drop by drop to etch out my plain face,
my angry tongue,
my softness that covers a violent chisel
and a torrent of anger at my existence; at the hypocrisy
and complacency of others' existence?

Caves exist because of what has been carved out of them.
Years of carrying away the earthy, stony
substance that now is an egg,
a crust, a rim
around chilly air.
And that is what I am. A rim
around some damp chilly air;
the water that carves my face—you know
what that is. No one has to talk of sorrow.
It weighs in the hands like pickaxes;
it pierces the ice of my childhood
and my children,
melted away from my life, eroded from my body.
These words—
               I give them names,

I send them to school,
I buy new shoes for them every six months
and darn their socks;
I read them stories at night

There is something about you
that I love.
A sense that you might be someone
I could have been,
were I not this empty damp cave you are exploring.
What does it mean to be born with empty hands?
Are we all born
with empty hands?
My anger is at the very cells my hands are made of;
instead of seeing them as whole, I see them
as being half there,
and I want to cut them off instead of leaving
ugly appendages.
I have made my caves
deeper than they were; I've dynamited them
beyond recognition. Foyers and vestibules of silence
still retain some of the delicate water's workmanship, but
hurt is a stairway, reaching farther down than
anyone can climb.

You spelunker,
find my father who deserted me and left an empty house, a leaky
                    boat
full of salt water——a sailor's daughter, afraid of water;
find my mother, a deep well, a fountain of tears,
a trickle of aimless molecules
trying to carve me up, cancel my existence,
instead creating a twisted 1,000-year-old column that doesn't
                    quite touch
any ceiling, that must stand alone,

for any effect at all;
find the men who have deserted me
left me in empty beds
with fingers empty of rings;
find my children whom I had to chisel out of my life
so that they might have better ones;
find my husband who battered at my head
trying to empty the brains out of it/

oh the caves of cold iron ore
I'm made of are so
empty/
there are days when I try to fill them with flowers,
with guitar strings,
with soft gold serpents
and I tease the spelunkers about the paths they will find;
but I cannot change
the fact
that I'm just a rim
around some damp chilly air;
and it makes me cry,
I never stop crying,
never stop carving myself away,
for the substance,
which I move farther and farther away from.
And I let you come in
because at least it is a moment of pretense
that there is something there
besides an angry hole,
a gap,
a cold empty place.

investigate my metaphors:
this open-heart surgery the world performs
on me,
counsel me, friends,
my letters,
they are all to men,
they reveal the woman
to a man,
they let you know what it's like to bleed
from the cunt,
an opening
to the world
you do not have.
                Counsel me,
I cannot cry any more. I have been hardened,
hurt, I am beyond love. I need
your love.
It is the only thing
that keeps a woman alive,
healthy, salty, salt
in the wound.

Dear Clayton,
You understand me better than any man.
You are
my twin. You are hard on me
to honor me, and kind
when there is a need for kindness. I sat, that Sat-
urday afternoon, telling you with my throbbing head from
too much cognac the night before
about the man I love,
the craftsman,
the mechanic,

who has rejected me,
refused, neurotically, to take me into
his life—how after months of absence I saw him again
and realized that
rationally
there are lots of men I find sexier than him,
many men who are more intelligent, more talented,
more interesting, more ambitious,
kinder, better men, and yet
when I am with him, I feel as if I belong
there, that it is a natural beautiful
reality; that I could never have that precise sense
with anyone else;
and paradoxically
that I think he feels that way with me too,
yet cannot honor the feeling in himself,
cannot let it serve him.
The hurt and hopelessness that overcomes me in the presence
of this recognition; worse, more
desperate than any war or murder or atrocity
could make me feel;
the failure
on such a simple level
of human responsiveness. And you are so kind to me,
good friend, poet,
reminding me so powerfully I cannot even cry
that it is easier to be kind to strangers
than to those we love.

Dear Jonathan,
Talking to you gave me more hope for communication
and more faith in myself
than Beethoven's Fifth Symphony ever has
(and we all know how much
I love

and need
Beethoven). You made my love and the hurt of
its rejection
by the mechanic
a powerful steel suspension bridge
on which we could walk beyond daily hurts and desires.
The knowledge that you probably are doing
the same masculine tap dance with another beautiful
woman, and she hurting and stinging as I do, she for you,
I for my mechanic, all my maternal instincts coming out
to protect another weary aching woman,
seemed only an academic proposition. While hurting her
you could understand me. Is there some awful
chain
we must perpetuate? No.
If you saw it as a chain, you would not
keep hammering new links. That is my hope,
then, that you are a better man than
the one I love. No daily consolation
in my own life
comes from that; but a sense of joy
that my missing sons and daughters will not have to
recapitulate
my history.

Dear Stan, I call you
my King of Spain, at times, because you seem to have
the sun pulsing, like a dying star, in your head.
And I would follow you anywhere
for that radiance, though I love another man,
the dirty mechanic
who cannot even walk, with pleasure, on a beach
because he is afraid to compete with the sun. How can I know
all his limitations, and still love him? Because love
is the part that breaks down in every machine;

because love is a crippled foot that makes you walk slower and
                          more
painfully; because love cannot win at the races;
because love is a kind of aristocracy
and it teaches, above all,
honor.

Dear Jacob,
Strongest man I've ever met,
only man I know who could have spent his life as a murderer for
the Mafia,
Kings are one thing. Gods another. You could
be a messenger from one of the gods—maybe my old
deified crony, George Washington—sent expressly
to show me
how hopelessly I love that mechanic,
and to remind me there's nothing unique about him
and what it means to be muscle-bound/ so strong
your muscles lock against themselves. Hey,
you love me rippling like antique moonlight over your
insulated life. Don't you.
But you ripple too,
like thick oil out of the Oklahoma ground,
crude and rich,
another version of steel,
and such a reminder,
a telegram from George himself saying
these men are too strong
to love a woman like you, one who keeps feeling
their biceps.
A friend tells me she can't believe
my image, that I really sleep all the time with a loaded gun
under my pillow. Well, she's right. If I could sleep with you
every night, that would really be sleeping
with a clean loaded gun.

A mutual friend of ours asks me
if I only like men who are hard to get; I reply,
thinking how inefficient the beautiful guns of the past were,
that I am attracted by challenges.
I realize, now, the differences between a man, a king, and one
                              of those
half-immortal heroes. I love the man;
I worship the king; and in the presence of the hero
I am improved, freed, lifted above my self in a kind of rational
oblivion to simple hurts. You, strong man, the hero,
you remind me of the toughness of my own life. And when I see
                              that
my hurt,
the sadness,
they don't go away;
but I also remember how happy I am
to be alive.

Dear Richard,
Maybe you are Beethoven. A reminder of how crazy,
self-destructive, and how beautiful
we all are.

Dear Shep,
bracelets locking me
to the past, I cannot speak to you
about my love for this other man, this mechanic,
because in your presence, it seems to have no power,
it seems small, and temperate, as feelings go,
the comfort and peace I feel with him, even with the knowledge
                              that
he has seen no way to accept me into his life, all those
feelings seem like dull woolen socks next to your flamboyance
and energy and the passion with which you would keep anyone
                   who exercised

123

the word love, chained to you. No, I won't talk to you
about anything. Talking to you, even thinking about you
is like setting my hair
on fire.

Dear Jan,
Our conversations are always literary.
You're one of the few men who take me seriously;
and I'll always remember your handsome face
as you flirt with another woman, a sweet good
friend of mine, saying Diane makes me wish I could
follow her around with a notebook and write down
everything she says. The story of my life. I
am a piece of paper; we could go into ecstasies about
texture and thickness of ankle, the writing surface
so smooth and muscleless/ the slightest pressure making
a mark on it. Jan, you remind me
of desperation. It is a drummer, a musician
with frantic energy, tapping and rolling, always
providing the tone or the tension. You
are desperate to play; the mechanic I love
is desperate to work. I, silly wild honeybee me,
I say I am desperate to love; but look at me
buzzing around, dancing, mating, all the dust of the world
clinging to my legs, trying to pretend it is pollen,
oh, if I really wanted to love, I would not choose
a loveless world in which to do it;
if I really wanted to love, would I choose a man
who believes there is no definition
for that word,
the only man I know who owns the complete
O.E.D., a work in which love must take up about
35 pages of derivation and usage.
Jan, you aways make me think things should be so much simpler;
just change. Just do it some other way, I think,

but the bee settles on the kitchen sink,
looking at a clear drop of water
on the white porcelain,
drums his wings, dances his drumming feet.
I have a nest of bees in my heart;
told that man I love I wanted to move to the country
and keep bees. Some might think that
a hostile gesture,
but remember, I was the child with gold strands in her hair,
in her braids, bees drumming the
yellow ribbons, convincing her
about beauty,
the honey of it,
worth a few stings
on smooth white skin.

Dear Hugh,
No, it's really you who's Beethoven, some sense in you
not allowing you to hear half of what is going on around you,
the music perhaps of your own powerful voice so strong
in your mathematical head, so loud,
you are insensitive
to anything else. For me, you
are a vibrating, live wire reminder
of the man I love; he can do anything with his hands
and he understands the working of most machines.
Your own hands are delicate,
should belong to a dancer, perhaps even a woman,
wave helplessly in the air as you talk.
Your beautiful face
of the lion looking over a dry dusty plain,
perhaps at a herd of running giraffe
in the distance,
allows me to sit and look at it for hours/ but you
would be a black lion

and all the fierceness in your hair
never reaches
even
your mouth,
and your shuffling feet, they do not even
inhabit the same world.
When I look at you
I always want to cry; then I get angry with myself
and am harsh and sharp with you
as a big brother would be to a skinny smaller one.
You need love so badly. Now shouldn't we be
able to get together? You, you remind me endlessly
that I do not want to love,
or loving you would be a natural gesture.
I want to share my life with that mechanic;
he makes me feel complete and peaceful inside; when I am
with him I am not the lion trapped, hunting for food
in a desert country that
both you and I become.
Love, what is it? a dry dusty day,
an engine that revs too fast, a knife with a blade it's
hopeless
to sharpen, a table with a broken leg,
oh love, you Hell's Angel with no bike to ride.

Dear Terry,
I like to think of you as the man who
might have left his wife
because of me. I, the protector, champion of wives,
hem and haw and get apologetic at this point; the hard part of me
knowing no man leaves his wife, really, because of
another woman but because of some internal struggle going on
inside himself that his wife begins to remind him of;
the soft part of me, having been left so many times,
hurting, wanting to help anyone who hurts, and at

126

the same time, turning a little spoiled
and wishing that sometimes it were I doing the hurting
and not I being hurt.
I would not sleep with you, even, saying I was going to
remain faithful to my mechanic, the man
who had thrown me out of his house, taken away the only
home I felt I had ever had, who had made me know
that if even he could feel this way about me, my life
was destined to be a maverick one, stray and lost,
that like those calves who wander away
I would probably die, fallen over a gorge or somewhere out
in the prairies with nothing to nourish me
and my hide not tough enough,
and no brand to even identify me.
But sleeping with you wasn't really
an issue; because
you are one of the few men I've ever met who believes in marriage,
who knows what faithfulness means, and who
really would have left your wife
if you had felt that I would have been a more proper one
for you.
But you are with her now,
and happily,
and constitute for me a dearness,
a reminder of goodness,
a kind of hope, sad as it sounds,
that once I almost inspired a man to love me so much
he
almost
changed his life
for me. What higher praise could
a woman have? And it does not assuage the wounds
I have sustained or really enlighten the fact
that without that one man I need,
the mechanic,

I will always be alone. He has sealed off
an empty cell in my brain. It is
a door that can never
be unlocked.

Dear M,
you ghost, you painful memory,
you original man for me, who let me sit and write my letters
while you used your electric saw, filling the room
with the smell of Vermont woods and my idea of home,
I grew up in a house full of women.
The only man in my life
was a piano
that I played lovingly;
a book I could take to bed and read;
a telegram that reminded me of my handsome uniformed father.
Oh, little girls
whose cunts are soft and hairless,
moist most of the time,
whose simple faces and wide pelvises
would take any father to bed,
you are tangled in your own poetry
and your husbands marry you away from the ocean,
are frightened by the angry waves in your eyes,
test you with their own deep mountain streams,
you sweet slippery fish who can exist in either salt water
or fresh, you are me,
and I love that innocent me who had to become tough
and give away her womanhood
and I love the toughest men in the world
because they can take my angry insistent voice
and shake it until again
it is sweet and high and clear
with the rosebush of my childhood
and my much happier children.

M, you are an initial

carved into my arm,
you are the model of every carpenter,
plumber, deep sea diver,
M for model,
you see what a Platonist I am,
and yes you are a painful memory, reminding
that M stands for man, and I have never been able to
really have the one "man" in my life
as much as I want. Oh, you cynics who say I carved my own initial
in my arm, that M is really an upsidedown W; but W is for
woman, the poet,
the calligrapher, and M for man, and after all,
that is what love is,
for all its trouble,
all its pain,
all its difficulty, it is a man
and a woman
who are opposites but cannot exist
without
each other. My arm
where your muscles are,
you strong men
that I love,
you mechanic and that of course is really what M stands for,
should proclaim to all the world
what poetry is
for this woman
this letter writer,
this passionate piece of paper
you will all
someday
read.

CONVERSATIONS WITH JAN

FIRST CONVERSATION

You grew up
in the country
a healthy childhood
happy
you say
too
You have a beautiful name, Jan Buchner,
but where has it all led you?
To an unlived-in apartment,
girls with false eyelashes,
and your childish temper.
Your eyes remember me
the way a fountain remembers

water

But I am desert water:
not easily found.
Only a rich man could pump me
through his
fountain.
This conversation
is a monologue.
I put you down/ at least your life
but dream of you at night.
cry
when you leave me alone.

SECOND CONVERSATION

Well,
why don't you follow me around
and take to heart,
    your valentine is between your legs,
all that I say?

You would rather
take a girl
with a pretty face
on a tour of your kitchen
than listen to me.
But I have lived with a torn heart
on my sleeve
for a long time
and I trail
blood from my eyes
wherever I go;
a final sign of death
when there has been violence
is blood
seeping from the mouth.

That is of course
what you listen to, Jan. The lesson of blood:
how bright it is when it's new;
but it fades fast
into a stain.

THIRD CONVERSATION

I am studying
sharks

I always think
of gamblers
as wearing sharkskin suits

This man I knew
stood on the street corner.
He was gambling with sharks.
He would put clothespins
on their tails
and see how far they would swim
before biting someone to death.

Am I talking to myself again,
or the sharks?

Does love ever get
any answers back
when it calls up a shark
on the telephone?

FOURTH CONVERSATION

snap-
dragons,
        do you know
what they are?

Flowers
the petals of which
children
open and close
like the jaws
of a
large biting animal.

They are
growing
outside the window
here;
and I am thinking of you,
imagining what you would say
if we were sitting in front of a fire
together
looking out the window
at these white
snap-
dragons
and I told you how my heart
snaps shut
on your finger,
my mind,
like a camera, clicks,
holds you inside
its film,

and outside the windows of white snowy danger
that keep us apart,
I look for
flowers.

FIFTH CONVERSATION

You terrify me.

More than the rattlesnake hissing in the corner
of the cabin
as I brush his tail with the heel
of my boot;

More than the thought of having my head sliced off,
as by the guillotine,
the one blink of the eyelids
which is supposed to occur
may mean that the brain knows exactly
what is happening,
blinks the eyes to see if it's true
cannot move the lips even an instant with the throat cut off/
that fear of knowing, even for a moment,
your head is in one place,
your body another;

More than falling into the coldest water;

more than
being alone at night in the woods.

You have it in your power

to do any of those things to me.

And you do it
with the same reflex
that makes me
scream.

SIXTH CONVERSATION

If I lived under the water
and shouted
my voice would make
such patterns on the sea
          as those
swirling
around me now.
You are thunder
You are the sound of the torrent which pounds through the canyon
You are more waves than my
          peacock voice could make;
fish in the sea
wet stone
a man I try to talk to
                    Words
like barracuda
replace love.

SEVENTH CONVERSATION

Imagination
only goes
so far.

135

Then fuel
is required.
How long
can a man talk to himself,
being both the questioner
and answerer,
without
finally realizing
he is
hopelessly
talking
to himself?
Your absence
has come home
to me
at last . . .
I can no longer bear
talking
to myself.

EIGHTH CONVERSATION

You
would not
believe
my existence
if there were not this
piece of paper
between us. The mountain
holds snow
the way
I hold
your hand. The higher

and colder
the longer
it remains
frozen—
    like a dinner without conversation
in the crevices
the deep ravines
with dry trees

The mailman
is to me
what the river was
to Li Po,
Thank God.
It moves too fast
to freeze.

NINTH CONVERSATION

The mountain
is the place
to meditate
on snow
      a frozen ocean
in which seals
cannot swim
The trees
grow
according to the slope
of the mountain
and into the shape

of the wind
         Snow
has no shape
I am snow
I am a mountain tree
I am the mountain
A frozen ocean
behind my eyes.

TENTH CONVERSATION

The Bengal tiger
with thick cushiony paws
and a motor
no mechanic
could fix
        ROARS
at me.

We both ask ourselves
why
in equally loud voices
sometimes sounding like automobile wrecks
clashing with the metal
of a hangover. I say,

   "Why do we always get drunk when we're together?"
   (I, despising the drunkard)
and you
      who like nothing better than getting
very drunk/

You with visions of Formula A cars
                          say,
          "Why do you remind me
          of something about my life I am afraid to,
          don't want to, think?"

This tiger
me
my belly a mass of deadly stripes
                    ROARS
at you
drummer
musician who beats on my brains.
Reminds you
that if you could ever be a man
you would not have to chase all those divers melodies.
Would not have to beat yourself to death.
Would be able to make music, or make time
at least
to go with my poetry.
                    But Bengal tigers
are man-eating
ferocious beasts
                and it is unlikely
that we two
will ever tame one,
be able to understand
what it means
those drunken mornings
              as the tiger roars painfully
              in our heads.

THE SHADOW OF THE EUROPEAN WHEEL

removed
from
my body
of life

the place where I am

                   separations

that occur
after an object
a life
has been conceived

           they are
wrenchings

         Those separations

which are
conceptual

the wheel   positioned
farther
out
(a matter of
style
I'm told)
      by mode
      of contrast

they do not
weaken
the structure

oh, yes,
my life with its
European wheel:
you

stretching out
in front of me

You lead.

You take me
everywhere
I want to go.

REMINDING ME OF YOUR OWN DEAD SEAS OF SILENCE

He liked his BMW
because it was
so quiet.
        Contrary to most
        bike riders
        who rev
        their engines
        shattering the full moon
        dripping pieces into the belt of my skirt.
        The night moon
        is replaced with your white helmet
            I see it
        rise on the road
        hardly a sound to remind me
        of your mouth
        on a dark night.

These are quiet objects:
        soft leather pants over wild asparagus in the summer
        your hand making a garden of my hair
        the sun tying my ankles around your hips
        my bare face after we have pressed oceans of the moon
        into the earth.

The machine
not running
reminds us of the difference between
quiet
and your own dead seas
of silence.

YOU, LETTING THE TREES STAND AS MY BETRAYER

You replaced the Douglas firs
    that reached
    like mechanics' hands
    outside my windows

    trying to understand the glass
    with furry, needle-tipped noses

You,
who understood me
in the rain

or at least
accepted me.

The trees never left
my windows
even when they put on gloves
for age;
they had married the glass
with the thud of falling cones.
They remembered my name
on windy nights.

But you
are my betrayer
who tried to frighten me with trees one night.
Then chopped them down
outside my windows
the next day

You ride a motorcycle
past wintry trees

and summer trees
and never once
think of me.
But my friends are
the falling branches
that will tilt you
and snap your neck one day.
I dream of your thick body
uprooted
and torn by a storm
on a motorcycle track.

You chopped down my trees—
they were my legs—
and unlike George Washington you did tell
many lies.
You are my betrayer,
you woodsman,
the man who stomps into the heart of this
forest.

MUSIC

can fill up my head like pneumonia

I have the ocean up to my shoulders.
You have your life.

This is the age of the tape recorder,
the photograph,

We hardly have any existence
but in records.

MY MARRIAGE CERTIFICATE

There are shadows
that look like dangerous smudges
on your lungs
filling up
a picture of you
I have in my mind.

GLASS

It was my horse——the old white nag——
who dragged your car out of the swamp.
Your sleek little black car was sunk 15 feet into the mud,
but we dragged you out.
The headlights were smashed, and the glass lost in the swamp;
but other than that everything seemed to be all right,
except, I have never quite been able to understand you since then.
It is as if we both are missing parts when we come together.
Perhaps it is better this way,
without communication on any level.
It prevents fuss.
How much was left at the bottom of the swamp?
How often your muddy footprints track through the 3rd door
where I live and where the oranges grow.
On my door is the sign GLASS
but anyone may come in.

I

Ride a cockhorse to Banbury Cross,
to see a fine lady upon a white horse.
With rings on her fingers and bells on her toes,
she shall have music wherever she goes.

In my room a hundred unopened letters lie on the glass table.
They have beautiful stamps on them from many countries.
When you come into the room, it is your privilege to open one
                              letter.
When Daniel first came to my room,
it was because he had stolen the key. I do not know whom he
                              stole it from,
but I know that he did not come by it rightfully.

146

He rode his horse up to my door,
as if he were a rider for the pony express.
He was dressed in brown leather
and lean. His horse was frothed from the ride.
He carried a leather pouch of letters.
They were all addressed to me. And he had ridden a great distance
to
bring them.
Now he comes once a month, dusty from the hot ride—
entering my corridors from another world,
the desert of Nevada, whose lakes are mirages,
the rough scrub country farther on,
and the foothills where stages used to pass
—I have always wondered how he got to my carpeted halls in the
1st place
He and the letters remind me once a month of other worlds;
the muddy footprints.

Otherwise, I might not know that any exist.

II

The 1st letter I open each mail shipment says the same thing,
"Do not forget to have your wrist watch repaired."
This comes in the form of a bill,
charging $85 for the repair of my watch.
However, as I have not owned a wrist watch in my entire life,
it always annoys me that I must pay such an enormous fee.
Often I wonder about time.
How did it pass when you were under the swamp in your car?
Did you hear your watch ticking?
Or your heart? while the snakes oozed by the windshield.
Sometimes I cannot bear to think about the past.

III

When my children were born, I gave them several gifts.
I gave the eldest a white pony and two gold wrist watches.
The exceeding inappropriateness of these 1st gifts was to haunt
                    me
until the birth of my second child.
My son fell under the hooves of his pony
and was crushed to death.
For some reason, still unknown to any of us,
the pony had swallowed both of the wrist watches just prior to the
accident.
We shot the pony and buried him in a separate grave.
I have always thought these last actions
to be unnecessarily cruel.
Since then, I have often thought about excesses of feeling
and how they injure others.

When my second child was born,
I gave it a box of seed pearls from Japan;
but the death of my first child still so tormented me
that I was not properly attentive to the second, a girl.
I left her playing with her box of seed pearls on the sidewalk one
                    day.
When I returned, she was gone.
The neighbor children were playing jacks
with the seed pearls and one of their own rubber balls.
They seem to play hopscotch more often than jacks now.

But I have never really felt that children were much more than
                    mistakes.

When I look into the mirror,
I know I say these things from excess of feeling.
If I were under the swamp,

sitting alone in the car where no one could see me,
I would not say these things.
I would have to admit death without reaching for the oranges.
I would have to say, "They have died because you willed them to
die."
I would have to say, "It is not that you are not beautiful—
because you are not.
It is not that you are bad,
because you are not.
It is your own answer, and it is your own punishment . . .
the oranges stolen away."
Under the swamp, sitting in your car
I hear the pony express riders
galloping away.
Daniel gone.
Even under the swamp
where the mud deadens everything,
I can hear them
riding away.
And I must say, "It is my answer, or it would not be so."

IV

Death does not mean very much more than the scattering of one's
belongings
So many times I have ridden the cockhorse to Banbury Cross
—the cock, riding the cock—
What is the relation of cock to clock?
death with bells,
rings on fingers waiting for music—the cock-clock crows—
and hearing nothing but laughter. Laughter is not good.
It is too easy to smooth everything with laughing.
Too easy to see you leave,
riding another cockhorse

and changing rings from one hand to the other.
Too easy to ride sidesaddle, laugh, and say,
"It was good while it lasted," or better,
"It was not good while it lasted."
One would go insane if it were not for the darkened room,
the cool, quiet.
Someday I will kill you for bringing those letters
each month,
riding the cocked-horse,
pony express;
your pony crushed my son under his hooves.
It is with the letter opener I fashion the keys to my room.
A glass letter knife. A glass key.
But the letters you bring—
they are paper.
The sun that made you sweat on the dusty ride was not my son.

V

The last letter I open each month comes from someone I would
                              rather
forget.
It is my uncle who owns a diamond factory.
He asks me to marry him.
How do you say no, and justify it, when somebody asks you
the very thing you want to be asked.
But the wrong person asks it.
So I put on a glass mask when I read my uncle's letters.
And he does not know what I mean.

VI

There are innumerable letters in the pile from people
I cannot understand.

These, I leave to be opened by visitors,
hoping they might shed some light on the matter.
On the day the mail arrives,
I wear every ring I own—five or six on each finger.
This makes it difficult to hold the letters,
and thus I feel calmer in doing so.
The absolute hate I feel for the mailman cannot be expressed.

VII

This is the first day I have been well enough to leave my bed.
For some weeks I cannot remember anything but bottles on the
                              medicine
table. I am told that I had a glass clock inside of me,
which had to be removed by a rather delicate operation.
Part of the difficulty lay in that the operation had to be performed
by a glass doctor who used only glass instruments.
Otherwise I might die.
However, in my mail shipment, a letter arrived saying,
"A glass man has been found."
Now that I am better, I am told what a serious malady I had.
Only two other men have ever suffered it,
and they both died on the operating table.

VIII

SWAMP

Have you ever seen a piece of glass in the mud?
It gets all smeared, but the minute you wash it in clear water
the mud dissolves away.
I feel that way every month when the letters come,
but I cannot shake off the idea that I have been sitting in your car

151

15 feet under the swamp.
And reading the letters reminds me of death & my age,
reminds me of my old body.
The young cowboy walking away
makes my old ring-covered fingers tremble over the paper.
I am an old piece of glass in the mud.
I hear the cocked-horse/ white nag/ the pony express
riding away.
The next black car
will be the inevitable one.
If I wear rings on every finger,
perhaps I can cover up my withering hands.
How often I think about time; the way it has ruined my life.
I am an old woman in silk, riding the cocked-horse.
Let me tell you,
when the sun dies, everything dies.

FIRE ISLAND POEM

for Jan

I resist
my banker
        He tried
to persuade me of the ocean
next to him.
        He whispers
in my ear
about the rustle of money
of the waves
that cut little sand cliffs out of the beach.
                I ride away

from him
with you,
        some launch cuts through my belly,
leaves scars like the stripes of tigers
to remind me
of deserted beaches, deserts in my life, men riding
their motorcycles in races
I could not qualify for.

Do you see how easily
I get tangled
           like my long hair whipping strangers on the deck
           of the boat taking us
           to a burning island,
how easily
a man with the sun burning in his hair
draws me
into his life? And how I run away from his
betrayals
        into the jukebox

153

into the rudder of the boat
into the broken heads of fish he cannot look at
into an ocean where sea turtles swim
into the sun,
on the beach
planting trees that will not grow,
desperately jumping into waves for the ritual
washing away
of memories
like gold glints of mica in the sand.

Open Me Up
and I will show you a mirror.
You are enticed by the mirror
and don't care about me.

My banker comes.
He rescues me during a midnight sunset.
He has a dark mustache
black
and reminds me that I have to light the way down
a deep road
with my pale skin,
my hands that flash with foam from the waves.
I would tear this page out of my book
and give it to you

If you knew
how
to accept it.

Not all fire burns you, young man.
Sometimes it comes in the shape of an island
or a tiger,
a woman,

like me,
who needs, wants,
cannot be
possessed.
Try,
just try,
to put fire
in your pocket safely,
young man.

QUICKSILVER SAILOR'S DAUGHTER

I will put the sign of quicksilver on my door.
It will take
the place of love.
Unfriendly faces look through
the windows
They remind me of the way you dance
You want at least three girls at once
and I am a reminder of your sailboat that you never sail.
Lightning
A burning boat
It moves across the water
burning scars across the water
but water
heals
the foam disappears leaving no sign
of a wound on the water.

How can quicksilver tell lightning
not to move so fast?

Woman is a wound.

You are not ready
to change your
definitions
Empty
unsailed
boat

                 And I am only
the alien daughter of
a sailor.

156

THE PINK DRESS

I could not wear that pink dress tonight.
The velvet one
lace tinting the cuffs with all
the coffee
of longing. My bare shoulder
slipping whiter
than foam
out of the night to remind me
of my own
vulnerability.

I could not wear that pink dress tonight
because it is a dress
that slips memories like
the hands
of obscene strangers
all over my body.
And in my fatigue I could not fight away the images
and their mean touching.

I couldn't wear that pink dress,
the velvet one you had made for me,
all year, you know.

I thought I would tonight because
once again
you have let me enter your house
and look at myself
some mornings
in your mirrors.
                But
I could not wear that pink dress tonight
because it reminded me

of everything
that hurts.
It reminded me of a whole year
during which
I wandered,
a gypsy,
and could not come into your house.
It reminded me of the picture of a blond girl
you took with you to Vermont
and shared your woods with.
The pretty face you left over your bed to stare
at me
and remind me
each night
that you preferred her face to mine,
and which you left there to stare at me
even when you saw how it
broke me,
my calm,
like a stick smashing across my own
plain, lonesome face,
and a face which you only
took down
from your wall
after I had mutilated it
and pushed pins in it to get those smug
smiling eyes off my cold
winter
body.

I couldn't wear that pink dress tonight
because it reminded me
of the girl who made it,
whom you slept with
last year while I was sitting in hotel rooms

wondering why I had to live
with a face
so stony no man could love it.

I could not wear that pink dress
because it reminded me
of how I camp on your doorstep now,
still a gypsy,
still a colorful imaginative beggar
in my pink dress,
building a fire in the landowner's
woods, and my own fierceness
that deserts me
when a man
no, when you,
show a little care and concern
for my presence.

I could not wear that pink dress tonight.
It betrayed all that was strong in me.
The leather boots I wear to stomp through the world
and remind everyone
of the silver and gold and diamonds
from fairy tales
glittering in their lives.
And of the heavy responsibility
we all must bear
just being so joyfully alive
just letting the blood take its own course
in intact vessels
in veins.
That pink dress betrayed my one favorite image
　　—the motorcyclist riding along the highway
　　　independent
　　　alone

exhilarated with movement
a blackbird
more beautiful than any white ones.

But I went off
not wearing the pink dress,
thinking how much I love you
and how if a woman loves a man who does not love her,
it is, as some good poet said,
a pain in the ass.
For both of them.

I went off thinking about all the girls
you preferred to me.
Leaving behind that dress,
remembering one of the colors
of pain
Remembering that my needs
affront you,
my face is not beautiful to you;
you would not share your woods with me.

And the irony
of my images.
That you are the motorcycle rider.
Not I.
I am perhaps,
at best,
the pink dress
thrown against the back
of the chair.
The dress I could not wear
tonight.